Cross-Currents

a guide to multicultural books for young people

ιΒbΥ

The International Board on Books for Young People was founded in the aftermath of World War II in the belief that children's books can foster international understanding. It is a non-profit organisation representing an international network of people from all over the world who are committed to bringing books and children together.

ιΒbΥ IRELAND

The Irish section was founded in 1998 with President Mary McAleese as its patron. IBBY Ireland's central aim is to promote access to books for young people everywhere – books with high literary and artistic merit – and in particular to reflect an international dimension to this work.

The organisation is engaged in developing links between Ireland and other countries in the area of children's books, and has hosted exhibitions and events presenting the work of illustrators and writers from many different countries. It has organised two conferences: one on interculturalism and multicultural children's books, and another on children's books in areas of conflict. IBBY Ireland is also involved in implementing and supporting the production of resources and has an active publishing programme. In 2001, it published *Changing Faces – Changing Places: A Guide to Multicultural Books for Children* and in 2002 re-published *A Bridge of Children's Books* (in conjunction with The O'Brien Press) the autobiography of Jella Lepman, founder of IBBY and the International Youth Library in Munich.

The board of IBBY Ireland is comprised of representatives from a number of organisations interested in children's books and reading in Ireland.

Cross-Currents

a guide to
multicultural books
for young people

Edited by

LIZ MORRIS *and* **SUSANNA COGHLAN**

*i*BbY IRELAND

First published 2005 by IBBY Ireland
c/o Ireland Literature Exchange/Idirmhalartán Litríocht Éireann, 25 Denzille Lane, Dublin 2, Ireland
Website: www.ibbyireland.ie

ISBN: 0-9541352-1-0

British Library Cataloguing-in-Publication Data
A catalogue record for this title is available from the British Library

1 2 3 4 5 6
05 06 07 08 09

IBBY Ireland receives assistance from

Typesetting, layout, design: kierannolan@oldtown.ie
Cover illustration: Alan Clarke
Printing: GraphyCems

The views expressed in the articles and reviews are those of the authors
and do not necessarily represent IBBY Ireland policy.

Illustrations are from book covers unless otherwise noted.
Thanks to An Gúm, Mentor, The O'Brien Press and Puffin Books for permission
to use copyrighted illustrative material in this book.

CONTENTS

In the book lists accompanying some articles, titles marked with an asterisk are reviewed in this publication.

ABOUT THE EDITORS

SUSANNA COGHLAN has been involved in the promotion of children's books and literacy in Ireland on a voluntary basis for a number of years, and has given talks on the selection and use of multicultural books to groups of teachers and librarians. Formerly treasurer of IBBY Ireland, she has been involved in organising IBBY conferences and events, and was a co-editor with Mary Fitzpatrick and Lucy O'Dea of IBBY Ireland's *Changing Faces – Changing Places: A Guide to Multicultural Books for Children* (2001). Over the course of the past year, Susanna taught in a public elementary school located in one of the most deprived areas of rural Cambodia. Prior to this, she worked for The O'Brien Press for a number of years.

LIZ MORRIS currently teaches in an Educate Together school with pupils from twenty-seven countries. She contributed both as author and editor to The O'Brien Reading Programme for Schools. A former president of the Children's Literature Association of Ireland, she was a board member of Children's Books Ireland for many years and is currently on the boards of the Reading Association of Ireland and of IBBY Ireland. She has administered the CBI/Bisto Book Awards and served on the judging panel. With Sarah Webb she has co-edited *BookFest*, the reading guide of the CBI Children's Book Festival, for the past four years. In 2005, she received the CBI Summer School Award in recognition of her contribution to children's books in Ireland.

ACKNOWLEDGEMENTS

IBBY Ireland would like to thank Séamus Cashman for editorial and production support and advice; Valerie Coghlan, Michael O'Brien and Geraldine O'Connor for fundraising and for on-going support; Ivan O'Brien for technical, production and other assistance and encouragement; Mags Walsh, Jenny Murray and James Curtin of CBI for all their help and support; the board of IBBY Ireland; all the people who reviewed the books, contributed articles or provided other assistance with this publication; thanks also for their contributions to Alan Clarke, Robert Dunbar, Eilís French and Kieran Nolan.

IBBY Ireland acknowledges with gratitude the support received from The Arts Council, Children's Books Ireland, The Church Education Society, The Church of Ireland College of Education, ESB Electric Aid, Joe Walsh Tours, Trócaire, INTO and Foras na Gaeilge towards the cost of producing *Cross-Currents*.

Thank you also to Phillip Butler, Valerie Coghlan, Rex Coghlan, Fergal Brady, Joanna Finegan, Shil Hanley, Íde Ní Laoghaire, Herbert Morris and Susan Morris. Special thanks to Alan Clarke for providing the illustration for the cover, to Kieran Nolan of Oldtown Design for his support and patience as well as for his design, typesetting and layout work, to Ursula Ní Dhálaigh for editing all the Irish language reviews, and to Sarah Webb for publicity, promotion and marketing.

FOREWORD

by Robert Dunbar

'TODAY THINGS ARE DIFFERENT and a modern successful Ireland is now a land of opportunity that attracts men and women from far and near.' This, according to a news item in *The Irish Times* of July 12, 2005, was part of an address given the previous day by President Mary McAleese to guests at a 'multicultural garden party', an event 'hosted by the President and her husband to celebrate the Republic's ethnic and cultural diversity.' A few weeks earlier, all primary schools in the Republic of Ireland had received a copy of *Intercultural Education in the Primary School*, designed, according to the cover, with the intention of 'enabling children to respect and celebrate diversity, to promote equality and challenge unfair discrimination.' The aspirations expressed here and in many recent similar political and educational utterances would, by most people, be considered highly laudable: the difficulty for all of us involved in these matters arises when the dream has to be translated into reality.

The blend of articles and reviews in *Cross-Currents*, which you are now reading, represents the latest attempt to facilitate the translation of the dream. IBBY Ireland deserve every congratulation for their initiative in seeing the venture through to its present attractive state and, even more so, for placing the emphasis of their endeavours on their belief in the value of story and fiction to illuminate existences, whether our own or those of other people.

While many teachers in Irish classrooms have long encouraged the reading of fiction and enabled children to approach literature in a way which can be genuinely mind-opening and liberating, they have often found themselves limited in their approach by material and methodologies. These, rather than provoking constructive discussion of the society in which our young people are growing up, have tended to endorse the values of that society and to focus almost exclusively on its more obvious stereotypes. The notion of a 'changing Ireland' may well itself have now become a commonplace but there still remain numerous opportunities for a wider interpretation of its possibilities. It would be difficult to imagine a teacher who would not find imaginative support in the pages that follow for a classroom approach in which fiction would have a central role in reminding us of the humanity we share beneath the apparent differences. The material and approaches advocated here will often bring with them a strong whiff of the new; the implication is of the need to reflect on our present classroom attitudes to fiction and story and, at the very least, to consider the possibilities of change. We must, however, be certain to ensure that what ultimately counts in such classroom transactions is the quality of the material, of the teaching and, especially here, our emphasis on the material as narrative. Understanding how writers shape their narratives to make works of art is a necessary step in understanding how those same narratives can subsequently shape our lives and those of our pupils.

This publication, *Cross-Currents*, deserves every possible success and I am very happy to recommend it to the attention of all engaged in the increasingly demanding (but highly rewarding) task of bringing books and young people together.

Robert Dunbar, formerly Head of English at the Church of Ireland College of Education, Dublin, is a commentator on children's books and reading.

CROSS-CURRENTS follows the acclaimed and influential *Changing Faces – Changing Places: A Guide to Multicultural Books for Children* (IBBY Ireland, 2001), and its articles and reviews continue to highlight the important role of books in promoting respect for human and cultural diversity.

Cross-Currents explores the significant role that books for young readers play in understanding an intercultural society: it also examines fluctuations in Irish society and takes a global perspective on education and development issues. Projects from locations as diverse as Nicaragua, Germany, Thailand, Alaska, Cambodia and France are described, many of the authors relating personal experiences of bringing books and stories to children in environments where books are scarce. Several of the articles suggest ways in which books can be used to foster intercultural communication and to enhance the teaching of global and development issues through stories and creative writing. Different and practical approaches to literacy and language development are also detailed.

A broad range of experiences, lifestyles, histories and heritages is reflected in the fiction, poetry, non-fiction and illustrated books reviewed in this guide. There are reviews of books for young readers of all ages, from infants to teenagers, published in Ireland and abroad over the past four years. It is heartening to note that the number of reviews of Irish-published books has increased from eight in *Changing Faces* to twenty-seven, which includes thirteen books in the Irish language. *Cross-Currents* also moves beyond the scope of its predecessor by including books originated and published in India and Africa.

The panel of reviewers and the authors of the articles reflect a wide and diverse range of experiences, but all share expertise and enthusiasm, and all give generously of both in this publication.

As the currents of social change and global development become increasingly interwoven, the need for young people to have access to books is vital: books educate in both a cultural and creative way, and they help to provide clarity of vision and understanding by naming and disentangling the complexities of experience. Books can provide an essential rite of passage in the global environment, an opportunity for subtle interpretation and broadening of horizons. We hope that *Cross-Currents* will be a useful starting point for all those interested in books for young people in our increasingly intercultural society.

The Editors

Race and Realism in Irish Writing

Irish writing and publishing for young people is struggling to keep pace with the rapid development of Ireland into a multicultural society. Valerie Coghlan examines how some Irish writers have responded to societal changes in their novels for young adults.

HOW WE DEAL with incomers to our shores is now a big issue in Ireland, and so an appropriate topic for 'realistic' fiction for young people. While solely issue-driven writing is not advocated, it may be asked if Irish writing and publishing take account of a changing society. So far, there are very few books featuring characters not of a 'traditional background', but recently there have been a few novels which address the situation of asylum seekers from African countries.

One of the first books published and set in Ireland and featuring a black character is John Quinn's *Duck and Swan* (1993). Duck, or Oduki, is about ten years old. Brought up in a children's home where he was mistreated, he is befriended by Emer, a girl who has family difficulties of her own, and by Granny Flynn, who gives Duck a temporary home. Following some name-calling, some of it to do with his colour, Duck becomes something of a local hero when he helps the town team win an important hurling match. It is largely a story of difference and acceptance, and Duck

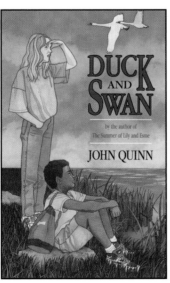

could have been different in a number of respects without essentially altering the story. That Duck is black is a device to heighten and make more obvious the fact that he is not a local boy.

Mark O'Sullivan's *White Lies* (1997) is a young adult novel set in an Irish country town. The plot centres on Nance's turbulent relationship with her boyfriend and, aris-

ing from this, her increasing interest in finding out more about her natural mother. Nance, born in Kenya, is of mixed race and was adopted by an Irish couple: until now, she has never tried to find out the details of her parentage. She is an intelligent girl, engaged with school, sport and a social life and too busy, she claims, to think much about her origins. And when a local drunk makes a disparaging remark about black Irish international footballer Paul McGrath, Nance empties a glass of Guinness over his head to the general approval of her friends. In *White Lies* race is relevant to the narrative but is not depicted as an issue. The focus lies on the mystery of Nance's birth.

The framing narrative in *The Love Bean* by Siobhán Parkinson (2002) concerns teenage twins, Julia and Lydia, who live in a prosperous part of Dublin. Parkinson's tone is light and she addresses with a degree of irony the racism in the twins' family and community that emerges when a group of black asylum-seekers comes to live next door. Both girls are immediately attracted to Tito, one of their new neighbours, and by the end of the book Julia has paired off with him. During the course of the novel Tito explains the repression from which he and others in the house have fled, giving readers a perspective on the circumstances that have led to the arrival of many asylum-seekers in Ireland.

The Love Bean also contains a parallel story, one that the twins are reading, which is set in early Celtic Ireland at a time when Roman invaders might have landed on the coast. Many of the circumstances and incidents in this story mirror those in Lydia's and Julia's story. Parkinson uses this device to point out that suspicion of newcomers is not a recent phenomenon.

Vincent McDonnell's *Out of the Flames* (2002) opens with the brutal murder of teenager Maria's mother by the soldiers of a corrupt regime in Malanga, a fictional African country. Sent to Ireland for her safety, she finds herself living with a group of asylum-seekers in a small village. David, a local boy, befriends Maria, but in doing so has to deal with the prejudice of the local community when a fire on his family's farm leads to violent actions. While Maria's pursuit by sinister members of the Malangan secret police and the narrative's ultimate resolution are implausible, *Out of the Flames* does give its readers a telling insight into the situation of those who flee from terrorism.

Prejudice is the underlying theme of Patrick Devaney's *Tribal Scars* (2004). It attempts to address far too many issues in its two hundred and five pages, and race is just one of these. But, while it has flaws, some due to bad editing, it is an attempt to represent some of the situations that confront people of non-traditional Irish background.

The narrative centres around Jakki and her teenage son Aidan. Jakki's father, a wealthy businessman, is horrified when his daughter falls in love with a black African medical student, has a baby with him and goes to Africa. Aidan's father becomes involved with a rebel movement, and, for their safety, Jakki and Aidan return to Ireland, where Aidan has to confront and come to terms with his background and his grandfather's prejudice. Other African asylum-seekers play subsidiary roles in the book. The title, *Tribal Scars*, can be taken to symbolise both the ritual scarring on the face of one of the characters, and the deep-rooted scars of prejudice and hostility in Irish society.

All of these books, in different ways, show Ireland as a changing society, not only ethnically but also socially and economically. But only the more recently published *The Love Bean*, *Out of the Flames* and *Tribal Scars* alert the reader to some of the matters underlying these changes.

We need to produce books in which society is shown, without remark, to be multi-racial and multi-ethnic

Books reflecting change and implicitly promoting understanding are welcome. Irish publishing is still a fledgling industry, and the number of new titles for young people published each year is small. We need to produce books in which society is shown, without remark, to be multi-racial and multi-ethnic, and in which characters from different backgrounds are depicted as a normal part of the landscape. Children's books can address a changing society and a changing world, and we hope through literature to encourage our children to regard these changes as enriching.

BOOKS DISCUSSED IN THIS ARTICLE:

Devaney, Patrick, *Tribal Scars*. Mentor Press, 2004, 1842102508*

McDonnell, Vincent, *Out of the Flames*. The O'Brien Press, 2002, 0862787645*

O'Sullivan, Mark, *White Lies*. Wolfhound Press, 1997, 0863275923

Parkinson, Siobhán *The Love Bean*. The O'Brien Press, 2002, 0862787726*

Quinn, John, *Duck and Swan*. Poolbeg Press, 1993, 1853713171

SARAH WEBB

Starting Early:
Multicultural Books for Babies and Toddlers

Early access to books featuring a wide range of people and places will give children a great start to their reading lives. Sarah Webb suggests ways to share time with babies and toddlers while enjoying a variety of intercultural books, from tried and tested classics to some recent publications.

IT IS NEVER too soon to start introducing babies to books. From their very earliest days, babies can enjoy looking at, touching and playing with books. Research shows that there is a strong connection between early book usage and later reading skills. As Dorothy Butler says in her groundbreaking book *Babies Need Books* (1995):

> Without the help of adults, a baby or small child has no chance at all of discovering books, of starting on the road to that unique association with the printed word which the mature reader knows and loves.

By making available to them a wide range of books featuring babies, toddlers and children from different cultural backgrounds, you are giving your babies or toddlers a great start to their reading lives.

The most important thing for this early age group is to make their first book experiences fun. Sharing time with Mum, Dad, a grandparent, or an older sibling, they can enjoy the playful antics of Helen Oxenbury's toddlers from different ethnic backgrounds as they tumble, dance, jump and play in her attractive board books such as *Clap Hands* (1998) and *All Fall Down* (1998). Books with lots of lively rhyme and repetition are particularly good for babies and toddlers. They can enjoy rhymes from a variety of cultures, such as Caribbean counting rhymes, American skipping rhymes,

Jewish prayers and Native American lullabies. Two recommended collections are *Under the Moon and Over the Sea: A Collection of Caribbean Poems* (2003), edited by John Agard and Grace Nichols, and *In Every Tiny Grain of Sand: A Child's Book of Prayers and Praise* (2001), collected by Reeve Lindberg.

The most important thing for this early age group is to make their first book experiences fun

Books also introduce young children to new experiences and other worlds in a safe and comforting manner. Some of the wonderful multicultural picture books offer a wide view of the world. In the Books for Keeps *Multicultural Guide to Children's Books* (1999), editor Rosemary Stones says:

> Whether you and your children, or the children you work with, live in the multicultural inner city or in the heart of the countryside, the talk, investigation and activity that can be engendered by fine picture books will lay good foundations for the development of informed and positive attitudes to racial identity – the child's own and that of other groups in our society.

Among some of the favourites in my own household are Janet and Allan Ahlberg's *The Baby's Catalogue* (2004) and *Peter's Chair* (1968) by Ezra Jack Keats, a classic American picture book. *So Much* (1996) by Trish Cooke and Helen Oxenbury is also a real winner: jaunty, rhythmic text combined with splendid and vivacious illustrations.

Make sure the books you use have clear, bright and child-friendly pictures

Interactive books are also popular – pop-ups, lift-the-flaps and tactile books make reading even more fun for babies and toddlers. Ken Wilson-Max has produced a great range of interactive books featuring a small black boy called Max. In *Max's Coin* (1999) Max has a sturdy cardboard 'coin', which he deposits in his wallet, in slot machines and into his money-box. The child is encouraged to read and play along with Max. Wilson-Max uses bold, flat colours combined with strong black outlines to create immensely appealing illustrations.

Make sure the books you use have clear, bright and child-friendly pictures. Look for durable board books that little hands and teeth can tear and chew. Place a 'book box' on the floor and allow your youngster to choose his or her own book.

Unfortunately, there are not many multicultural board books or interactive books available at the moment, but hopefully more will be published in the near future. As a parent, you can encourage this by actively seeking out and buying multicultural books for your children and supporting publishers who are producing books featuring children with different ethnic backgrounds.

Ask your local bookseller or librarian for help; they can often suggest suitable titles or order books for you if they don't have them on their shelves.

BOOKS DISCUSSED IN THIS ARTICLE:

Agard, Joan and Grace Nichols, *Under the Moon and Over the Sea*. Walker Books, 2003, 0744598427*

Ahlberg, Janet and Allan, *The Baby's Catalogue*. Puffin Books, 2004, 0140503854

Butler, Dorothy, *Babies Need Books*. Penguin Books, 1995, 0140156798

Cooke, Trish and Helen Oxenbury, *So Much*. Walker Books, 1996, 0744543967

Keats, Ezra Jack, *Peter's Chair*. Puffin Books, 1998, 0140564411

Lindbergh, Reeve, *In Every Grain of Sand*. Walker Books, 2001, 0744582326

Oxenbury, Helen, *All Fall Down*. Walker Books, 1998, 0744555841

Oxenbury, Helen, *Clap Hands*. Walker Books, 1998, 0744561027

Wilson-Max, Ken *Max's Coin*. Chrysalis Children's Books, 1999, 185602282X

Stones, Rosemary (ed.), *Books for Keeps Multicultural Guide to Children's Books*. Books for Keeps, 1999

A Balloon for Grandad

Nigel Gray, illustrated by Jane Ray
Orchard Books, ISBN 2-84362-102-9, £4.99 (pbk)

Sam has a lovely big red balloon that escapes out the open back door and floats off into the city sky 'like a tiny red berry'. The wind takes his balloon and blows it south towards the mountains. To ease his loss, Sam's dad tells him where the balloon is going. We follow its journey to where Grandad Abdullah lives on an island, looking after his goats and date trees, and the balloon becomes a way for Sam to feel a connection with his grandfather. The illustrations depict different ways of living and provide an opportunity to talk about diversity of houses, climates and animals. Sam's family has a range of different skin tones, which might raise interesting questions about family likenesses and identity. There is also an important message about children staying connected with grandparents living far away, perhaps in a different country or culture, and how parents can help support this relationship.

AO'D

African Animals ABC

Philippa-Alys Browne
Barefoot Books, ISBN 1-898000-53-0, £5.99 (pbk)

This is a stunningly illustrated picture book for young children. Its author and illustrator is an African artist from Zimbabwe. The book adopts an alphabetical approach to introduce a range of large and small animals of Africa. Each page has a short narrative and supporting pictures conveying information that will easily engage younger children – for example, crocodile snaps and rhino stomps. It is the quite beautiful watercolour images of animals and their surroundings that set this book apart. These images are striking in the colours, textures and tribal patterns they convey. They depict animals in their natural world; every blade of grass, every leaf and animal coat, has been covered in painstakingly detailed patterns. The vivid colours and striking contrasts convey a landscape of sunshine and shade that brings the world of African animals to life. A useful glossary of nature notes on each animal is provided.

GO'C

An African Princess

Lyra Edmonds, illustrated by Anne Wilson
Picture Corgi, ISBN 0-552-55033-7, £5.99 (pbk)

'My name is Lyra and I am an African princess.' So begins this multi-layered picture book, based on the author's own life. Lyra is teased at school for looking different and being different. Her mum is African and her dad is white with red hair and freckles – Irish, perhaps? Lyra, who also has freckles, lives on the tenth floor of an apartment block, unlike the other children, who live in houses. Lyra's mama tells her to hold her head up high because, also unlike her school friends, she's an African princess. But Lyra doesn't believe her, until one day she visits Africa for herself and meets her special aunt, Taunte May. 'Remember to be proud of who you are' is Taunte May's advice, and this time Lyra listens. The mixed-media illustrations are full of authentic detail, the pages singing with bright yellows, reds and greens. Wilson uses many different techniques, from collage to screen-printing, cleverly layering each immaculately designed page. Highly recommended.

AN AFRICAN PRINCESS

SW

A Present for Paul

Bernard Ashley, illustrated by David Mitchell
HarperCollins, ISBN 0-00-664160-1, £4.99 (pbk)

All children fear being lost, while losing them is their parents' biggest worry. Ashley tackles this nightmare scenario with just the right balance of anxiety and relief. Pleasure, shopping in the busy market with her dad, takes her hand from his for just a second as she looks for a present for her brother Paul, who needs a teething ring. When she turns around, Dad has vanished. Struggling not to panic, because her dad calls her a big grown-up girl, she sets about finding him, but becomes more and more frightened. All comes right, before her father has even had time to miss her. Mitchell's energetic illustrations perfectly integrate with the story, and it's fun to see the different shoppers reappear again and again in the background, completely oblivious to Pleasure's problem.

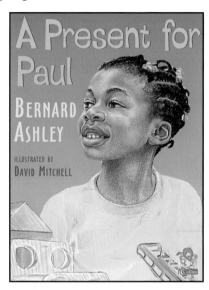

CC

Billy and Belle

Sarah Garland
Frances Lincoln, ISBN 1-84507-038-0, £5.99 (pbk)

Billy lies in bed thinking about his hamster, and about the new baby that will soon be born in his family. His sister Belle is too young for school, but when Mum goes to hospital to have the baby, Belle accompanies Billy to school and is very excited. It is Pet Day, and she wreaks havoc in Billy's class when she tiptoes outside to check the number of legs on a spider. Later that night, as Billy lies in bed thinking, Dad arrives home with Mum and their new baby brother. There is little suspense in the storyline and the illustrations are somewhat fussy, but small children will love the warm endpapers and the chaotic scenes in the playground when all the pets escape. This book may give rise to questions about families and about how babies are born, and would be welcome in most homes and in junior classes in school.

JMa

Bringing the Rain to Kapiti Plain

Verna Aardema, illustrated by Beatriz Vidal
Macmillan, ISBN 0-333-35164-9, £4.99 (pbk)

The flow of words in this classic picture book conveys the intensity of waiting for rain to fall on an arid African plain. In 'House that Jack Built' format, the words build and build as we watch with herdsman Ki-pat for drops to fall from the gathering clouds. And when the drought persists, Ki-pat – listening to his cows, who 'mooed for the rain to fall from the sky' – decides to act. An arrow shot from the bow he puts together punctures the cloud and releases the rain that restores green grass to Kapiti Plain. And Ki-pat's reward? A wife and a little Ki-pat. The illustrations are gentle and slightly stylised watercolours, dovetailing exquisitely with the words to bring the mood of Africa to a very young audience. All children should know this book.

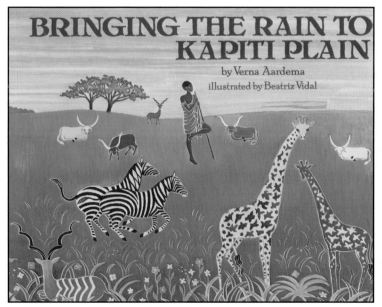

VC

Chameleon Races

Laura Hambleton
Milet, ISBN 1-84059-422-5, £5.99 (board)

Hambleton's delightful Chameleon proposes a race to his lizard friends, but there is more co-operation than competition as they all enthusiastically join in. Gecko rides a bicycle, Gila Monster skips and Iguana gets out the roller skates. Across the pages they hop, skip, jump and run, through the river, up the mountains and over the rocks, and all arrive at the finishing point simultaneously. The vivid images on each page are composed of collage and paint, giving a sense of the hot environment of the reptiles in a book that is a real must for young readers.

It is also available in thirteen different bilingual editions, including English with Arabic, Chinese, French, Turkish or Vietnamese. There is a companion volume, *Chameleon Swims*, 1-84059-435-7.

CHAMELEON SWIMS

vc

Frog and the Stranger

Max Velthuijs
Andersen Press, ISBN 0-86264-625-1, £4.99 (pbk)

Animals have long been used by picture-book-makers to stand in for child protagonists, given the potential for ambiguity and the evasion of issues of gender and race, but here Max Velthuijs uses his animal protagonists to look at prejudice directly. Rat sets up camp at the edge of the woods: '"You have to be careful of rats," said Duck. "They're a thieving lot." "How do you know?" asked Frog. "Everyone knows," said Duck indignantly.' Frog is not so sure. As the story progresses, antagonism is built up through fear and rumour; and, while there are a few voices of reason, these face the disapproval of their peers for extending a welcome to the stranger. Eventually Rat, who is industrious if a little scruffy, helps the community and is accepted – ironically, at the point when he has decided to move on. '"Perhaps I'll come back one day," said Rat cheerfully. "Then I'll build a bridge across the river."' Clarity of emotion expressed in such deft language, together with illustrations that have a childlike quality and are remarkable for their painterly subtlety, make this a book not to be missed.

LJ

Elmer and the Hippos

David McKee
Red Fox, ISBN 0-09-945114-X, £4.99 (pbk)

Elmer, David McKee's much-loved patchwork elephant (whose fans will know that he knows something about celebration of difference), is presented with a problem when three angry elephants come to see him complaining that the hippos have come to live in their river. They want Elmer to make the hippos go away. When Elmer goes to see the hippos, one of them says that they know they are not wanted, but that their own river has dried up. Elmer appeals to the elephants' self-interest when he asks them to 'Imagine if our river dried up' before going to see for himself what has happened to the hippos' river. Clearly about displacement of peoples, this book is thoughtful both in its exposition of attitudes and in its contemporary reflections on aid. Elmer goes to the root of the problem when he finds out why the river has dried up, and he enlists the practical help of the elephants, who work with the hippos to get the water flowing again. This is a book with a warm message that arises quite naturally through a satisfying narrative, and is one that should be in every nursery and infant class – indeed, in every home.

LJ

Full, Full, Full of Love

Trish Cooke, illustrated by Paul Howard
Walker Books, ISBN 1-84428-782-3, £4.99 (pbk)

The atmosphere of this book by award-winning author Trish Cooke is effectively conveyed in the title. Jay Jay spends Sunday with Grannie, and while she prepares dinner he waits hungrily for family and friends to arrive. The description of the meal and its many dishes, and the scene of a large, happy family enjoying it, convey a warm, affectionate atmosphere of comfort and security. The playful rhythm and rhymes of the text echo this joyful tone. Jay Jay's world is indeed full of love, and his close relationship with Grannie is beautifully illustrated in words and images. The strong, colourful drawings by Paul Howard are full of detail, showing Grannie's well-stocked kitchen and evocatively mirroring the feeling of plenty and warmth throughout the book. The reader will leave this book as satisfied and happy as Jay Jay and his family.

JFi

Heads, Shoulders, Knees and Toes

Annie Kubler
Mantra Lingua, ISBN 1-84444-145-8 Arabic/English, £6.50 (board)

A charming book featuring hosts of different toddlers from various ethnic backgrounds, all dancing and playing along to the well-known rhyme of the title. Each page shows a toddler demonstrating one of the actions – a small black boy touches his toes, a small orange-haired girl touches her mouth and so on – but the very young will especially love the animals that mimic the toddlers' actions. The illustrations are bright and child-friendly, making this a great choice for active toddlers. Also available in English with Albanian, Bengali, Chinese, Farsi, French, Gujarati, Panjabi, Portuguese, Somali, Spanish, Tamil, Turkish or Urdu.

SW

Handa's Hen

Eileen Browne
Mantra Lingua, ISBN 1-84444-075-3 Croatian/English, £7.50 (pbk)

In this vibrant picture book, Handa is assisted by her friend Akeyo in her search for Grandma's missing black hen. On their journey the girls discover a variety of wild creatures, all of which appear more homey than wild. *Handa's Hen* familiarises the very young child with numbers, but it also evokes the harmonious, communal world of the Lou tribe in south-west Kenya. The variety of colour in the illustrations is most attractive: we journey from the predominantly ochre hues of the compound to a more exotic landscape, reflecting the excitement of the girls' quest. Equally appealing is the simplicity of the text: its direct speech and repetition ensure the book's accessibility for the young listener. This is essentially a celebratory book. It is joyful in its luscious colour and animated facial expressions. Both the mystery of birth and the wonder of difference are celebrated, especially when Grandma's black hen miraculously produces a brood of different colours! *Handa's Hen* is available in twenty other dual-language editions – English with Albanian, Arabic, Bengali, Chinese, Farsi, French, Gujarati, Hindi, Italian, Panjabi, Portuguese, Russian, Shona, Somali, Swahili, Tamil, Turkish, Urdu, Vietnamese or Yoruba – and in big-book format in English only.

ÁNicG

I Don't Eat Toothpaste Anymore

Karen King, illustrated by Lynne Willey
Tamarind Press, ISBN 1-870516-16-8, £4.50 (pbk)

'I used to be a baby. But I'm big now.' So begins this delightful picture book for younger children of two and up. Abiola is a 'big girl' now and can dress herself, wash herself and tidy her own bedroom. Still, she's never too big for a hug! The colourful, realistic watercolour illustrations by Lynne Willey will really appeal to very young children.

I DON'T EAT TOOTHPASTE ANYMORE

SW

If You Go Walking in Tiger Wood

Alan Durant, illustrated by Debbie Boon
HarperCollins, ISBN 0-00-710390-5, £5.99 (pbk)

This beautifully produced peep-hole book has an unusual front cover with no type whatsoever: it features simply a tiger print, with a square cut-out window and a friendly tiger face peering through. Each double spread is a feast of rich, colourful jungle leaves and exotic foliage that puts the reader right in the middle of this jungle-wood with the two protagonist children: a little girl and (perhaps) a younger brother, who holds on to her arm or clothes as they wander tentatively through the wood. Each peep-hole on the right-hand page has a set of eyes that might belong to a tiger. But as the page turns to reveal a friendly animal, this same peep-hole frames the partly hidden tiger, who is behind the children all the time. The reader is aware of the frightening fact that the children are always being watched.

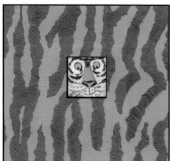

This book is an exciting introduction to the fact that, for children living in other parts of the world, the possibility of meeting these animals in the wood is a reality.

PO'D

I Love You

photographs by David Ellwand
Amazing Baby (an imprint of Templar), ISBN 1-59223-232-9, £12.99 (board)

This giant-sized board book features babies from different cultural backgrounds. Each child is photographed in striking black and white, and there is simple text accompanying each image: 'Tiny nose and tiny toes. Funny faces, tickly places. Tickle, tickle.' There is a slot on the last page to hold your own baby's picture. This is a charming book for younger children and an attractive addition to any nursery bookshelf.

SW

Let's Feed the Ducks

Pamela Venus
Tamarind Press, ISBN 1-870516-53-2, £3.99 (board)

Max wants to go and feed the ducks in the local park, so he puts on his red wellies and grabs his dad by the hand, and off they go. Along the way they meet lots of Max's friends and pass through the market, where produce from many different parts of the world is being sold, before finally reaching the park where the ducks are waiting. This hand-sized board book with child-friendly rounded edges is a gentle and reassuring read. Each double-page spread features scenes from Max's daily life – from the market to the children playing in the playground and the mice in the pet-shop window – just the kind of things that interest every toddler. The watercolour and pencil illustrations are full of vibrant colour, and are pitched just right for younger readers. An ideal first book.

SW

Not So Fast Songololo

Niki Daly
Frances Lincoln, ISBN 0-7112-1765-3, £5.99 (pbk)

A beautiful South African story of the strong bond between a young boy, Shepherd, and his grandmother Gogo, who is old and whose face 'shines like new shoes'. While on a shopping expedition in the city, Shepherd entertains Gran with his games so that she will not be afraid of the crowds or the bus journey. As he waits for Gran to do her shopping, he sees some red runners (or 'tackies') in a shop window. His own tackies, having once belonged to his older brother, have holes in the soles. Though free to look and long for new ones, he cannot have them, as there is no money for such things. Happily, Gogo has other ideas: she wants to reward him for helping her with the shopping and for keeping her safe in the big city. Shepherd is delighted with his gift of new tackies with red stripes, and, as he strides out of the shop with his head held high, she calls, 'Not so fast, Songololo' – her favourite name for him. The vibrant illustrations perfectly reflect the life and colours of the city and the love and affection between the pair as they wander in and out of shops and streets.

CC

The Swirling Hijaab

Na'ima bint Robert, illustrated by Nilesh Mistry
Mantra Lingua, ISBN 1-852691-638 Farsi/English, £7.50 (pbk)

In this delightful picture book, the *hijaab* becomes a multi-purpose object that allows a young girl to embark on flights of fantasy. She can imagine herself in exotic locations such as the desert and the high seas, and in more familiar situations such as picnicking in the park or resting on the couch at home. This book seamlessly bridges Eastern and Western influences, subtly informing us that, despite the different beliefs and traditions in different parts of the world, emotional needs for comfort and love are the same everywhere. The gentle, rounded illustrations introduce some of the cultural and religious aspects of the Muslim tradition in a very appealing way. Also available in English with Albanian, Arabic, Bengali, Chinese, Czech, French, Gujarati, German, Italian, Malay, Panjabi, Pushtu, Portuguese, Serbo-Croat, Somali, Spanish, Tamil, Turkish or Urdu.

AMK

The Best Mum

Sarah Nash, illustrated by Pamela Venus
Tamarind Press, ISBN 1-870516-62-1, £4.50 (pbk)

A parent at the school gates asks Kizzy's mum what work she does, and she replies that she doesn't work. Thankfully, Kizzy knows this is very far from the truth. This is a story for mums to read and enjoy in quiet moments with their children – dads might want to change just a few words at the very beginning and end! The illustrations are vivid, colourful and full of detail and provide a great stimulus for discussion. The language is full of imagery, similes and fun, and children could come up with endless variations on the theme as they think of ways their parent might describe them.

JMa

Tickle Tickle

Dakari Hru, illustrated by Ken Wilson-Max
Bloomsbury, ISBN 0-7475-6027-7, £4.99 (pbk)

A simple concept – a father tickling his baby son – is turned into a sheer tour de force on many levels. First there is the language, wonderfully lyrical and almost hypnotically rhythmic in the voice of the delighted child: 'me papa tickle me feet.' Add to that the magic of Ken Wilson-Max's fabulously evocative pictures, which show the child's sheer joy in the play with his father. The presence of wonderfully positive images of the father, all too often absent in picture books for younger children, is also worth noting. The images are big and presented in vivid colour. The father's love for his son and the joy he is getting from the tickling game are drawn beautifully in both the text and the images. Irresistible.

FO'S

Using Fiction in Development and Intercultural Education (DICE)

Development and intercultural education is becoming an increasingly important part of the Irish primary school curriculum. Barbara O'Toole presents some of the methods recommended by the DICE project for incorporating books into teaching strategies.

UNDERSTANDING and appreciating difference and diversity is at the heart of the DICE project. Working with groups of student teachers, DICE provides a suggested framework for applying the principles and content of development education and intercultural education across the curriculum. The following article looks at some strategies recommended by DICE for integrating books into the teaching of development and intercultural education.

This ability to take on another person's perspective is the essence of intercultural communication

Development education focuses on global issues – the interdependence of all peoples; issues of trade, aid and poverty; environmental sustainability; the impact of globalisation on local communities, and so on. Intercultural education focuses more on 'local' issues – the increasing diversity of Irish society and classrooms, and the need for interaction and engagement between communities.

DICE NOTICEBOARD

In both development and intercultural education we are asking children, not just to acknowledge lives and cultures different from their own, but to begin to develop the ability to 'take the perspective of the other', whether 'other' is someone from another culture in the classroom or someone on the other side of the planet. This ability to take on another person's perspective is the essence of intercultural communication. It requires the ability to empathise, to imaginatively enter the emotional experience of another. According to the Irish primary-school curriculum, empathy is one of the key skills that children will develop during their primary education. The guidelines for Social, Personal and Health Education state:

> Developing empathy is (also) fostered at all levels in the school, as it is essential for handling and managing relationships, promoting compassion and sensitivity, and appreciating diversity. (Page 12, *Teacher Guidelines*, SPHE)

In this, literature plays a key role: it opens the door to different worlds and enables children to enter the emotional experiences of individuals who may have very different lives from theirs. Some books do this in a direct way, through stories exploring children's experiences of complex and traumatic events. For example, *Rose Blanche* (1985), by Roberto Innocenti and Ian McEwan, explores life in wartime Germany, where a young girl discovers a concentration camp on the edge of her village. *Sami and the Times of the Troubles* (1992), by Florence Parry Heide, Judith Heide Gilliland and Tim Lewin, is the story of a family living in Beirut. Through the text and vivid illustrations, the book captures ordinary aspects of a child's life in the midst of an extraordinary time. It also powerfully conveys the similarities between all our lives – showing how Sami continues to look for opportunities to play and to spend time with his friends and family, even in the midst of war. In looking at situations very different from their own, in books and stories, children can be struck by the similarities in people's lives and come to realise that our commonalities are as important as our differences.

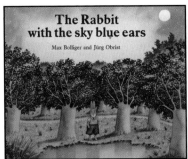

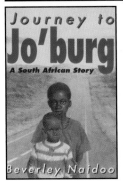

Thus, issues of belonging, of visible differences, of being a newcomer, or of having a new member arrive in the community can be explored in non-threatening ways

Often, with younger children, picture books that explore complex issues in indirect ways can be very useful. When I worked as a Special Needs teacher in the United Kingdom with children who had behavioural and learning difficulties, I sometimes used an educational therapy approach, which is a means of working with children who have emotional blocks to learning.[1] Here, stories proved a useful 'way in' to looking at difficult emotional issues, but at one remove and therefore safely. I have also found this approach useful with issues of difference and diversity. *Elmer* (1989) by David McKee looks at an elephant with a difference – 'Elmer was not elephant colour'. *The Rabbit with the Sky Blue Ears* (1988) by Max Bolliger and Jurg Obrist has a similar theme. A particular favourite of mine is *What If?* (1997), by AH Benjamin and Jane Chapman, about a kangaroo who arrives on a farm, sparking alarm amongst the animals who have no idea what a kangaroo can do and worry they may lose their place on the farm. Thus, issues of belonging, of visible differences, of being a newcomer, or of having a new member arrive in the community can be explored in non-threatening ways.

To mark International Day Against Racism, the DICE project, in conjunction with the librarian of the Church of Ireland College in Rathmines and a college lecturer, organised a display of children's books that explore themes of difference and similarities, diversity and race. International Day Against Racism was set up to commemorate the Sharpeville shootings in South Africa in 1960, so it is perhaps not surprising that Beverley Naidoo's work features strongly in this collection. I have found that her books really engage older children (fifth- and sixth-class level and above), and I used extracts of Nelson Mandela's *Long Walk to Freedom* (1994) as supplementary material to *Journey to Jo'burg* (1985) with a class of twelve-year-olds.

While there are many practical factors to bear in mind when choosing books for the class library – such as age-appropriateness, balance of factual books and fiction, books showing gender balance, positive ethnic role models and so on – another suggestion is to have a number of books available that encourage children to empathise with the experience of others. These can enhance the teaching of development and intercultural education in a unique way, allowing children to enter other worlds, facilitating their ability to appreciate the lives and situations of others, and helping them to understand that, although life circumstances may differ, all children have similar wants, needs and human rights. Thus the 'global' becomes 'local', enabling solidarity and understanding between people, whether within Ireland or between children in this country and communities overseas.

THE 'DICE (DEVELOPMENT AND INTERCULTURAL EDUCATION) PROJECT'

DICE runs courses for student teachers in the colleges of education. Over the last three years almost 1000 students in four of the five colleges have participated in courses that aim to explore key concepts and teaching strategies in development and intercultural education. (Coláiste Mhuire, Marino; Froebel College of Education, Blackrock; St Patrick's College, Drumcondra; The Church of Ireland College of Education, Rathmines. DICE also has links with Mary Immaculate College in Limerick.)

The 'DICE Project' was recently awarded the *World Aware Education Award* by the North-South Centre of the Council of Europe.

DICE is a partnership project of Development Cooperation Ireland at the Department of Foreign Affairs.

The views expressed in this article are those of DICE and can in no way be taken to reflect the official opinion of DCI.

BOOKS DISCUSSED IN THIS ARTICLE:

Innocenti, Roberto and Ian McEwan, *Rose Blanche*. Red Fox, 2004, 0099439506

Heide, Florence Parry, Judith Heide Gilliland and Ted Lewin, *Sami and the Times of the Troubles*. Houghton Mifflin, 1995, 0395720850

McKee, David, *Elmer*. Andersen Press, 1989, 0862642086

Bolliger, Max and Jurg Obrist, *The Rabbit with the Sky Blue Ears*. Canongate Books, 1988, 0862412048

Benjamin, AH and Jane Chapman, *What If?* Little Tiger Press, 1997, 1854304038

Mandela, Nelson, *Long Walk to Freedom*. Little Brown, 1994, 0316874965

Naidoo, Beverley, *Journey to Jo'burg*. Collins, 1999, 0006754554*

[1] Caspari Foundation – www.caspari.org.uk – for more information on Educational Therapy

LesArt
A Children's Reading Project from Germany

Berlin's LesArt provides a child-centred space where children can enjoy a range of activities inspired by books, from storytelling to sleepovers.

I N A RATHER QUIET STREET on the eastern side of Berlin is a rather quiet, ordinary-looking house. From the outside, it looks as if maybe there's a kids' crèche or play-group on the ground floor – cottonwoolly things stuck on the window, streamers, glitter, that kind of giveaway. When you go inside, it's still quite an ordinary house – except that every room seems to be a playroom-*cum*-library. Everywhere are signs of children and books: children's illustrations cover the walls, illustrators' illustrations too; books spill out of bookcases (well, actually, no, they don't – this is Germany, after all – but you do feel there are a lot of books, all the same): there are inviting corners in which to huddle with your book, space in which to stretch out and read, space in which to paint and potter and make a book-related mess, open areas in which to sit and listen. And, best of all, at the top of the house are two cosy dormitories – only without beds, just mattresses and cushions, you bring your own sleeping bag – with giant papier-mâché witches and hobgoblins and bats that would keep any adult awake, hovering over doors and skulking in corners.

Sabine Mähne's passionate commitment to engaging children with books is what sustains this place

Sabine Mähne, who runs this amazing place, is very proud of the dormitories. 'Do you know, we hardly ever need to paint these rooms,' she says. 'Every other room in the house gets repainted from time to time, but these rooms just seem to stay clean and fresh.' She puts it down to the effect of giving children their own environment to be in and to look after, an environment so child-friendly and fun that no child would dream of scribbling on the walls or scuffing the doors.

Sabine Mähne's passionate commitment to engaging chil-dren with books is what sustains this place, and this project – dedicated to bringing books alive for children, all children, including those who come from homes where books are not part of the furniture.

LesArt works exclusively with the classics of German and world literature, with a special emphasis on folk- and fairytales, and with books nominated for the German children's book-prizes, which are awarded every year (by the equivalent of Children's Books Ireland) and divided very sensibly into the categories of picture book, children's novel, young adult novel and information book, with an extra category of best book chosen by a children's jury. Popular reads are fine, in LesArt's view, but nobody needs an organisation like LesArt to find books like that: the short-listed books represent the best books published in Germany each year, and LesArt is about introducing children to the best books.

Once a month, children come with their sleeping bags and a couple of euro to pay for their breakfast, and camp out here

But it is how LesArt goes about effecting these introduc-tions that makes its work so special. LesArt's work centres directly on the books themselves. The people here are mostly artists, rather than writers, who work with children to engage their imaginations through painting, drawing and making things inspired by books. Authors are invited in to meet the children from time to time, but the emphasis is on getting the children to relate to the books, not to the personalities of those who write them.

LesArt's 'sleepovers' are its most famous activity. Once a month, children come with their sleeping bags and a couple of euro to pay for their breakfast, and camp out here. Before they go to bed, there's an adventure out in the night city – hunting for elves or magic objects to break a wicked spell in the city's parks, up trees, and around fountains, if the chil-dren are young – or looking for literary landmarks for the more sophisticated readers. Then it's back to the LesArt house with the booty, for a late-night book-related activity over the cocoa, and then off to the Land of Nod, supervised by all those spooky characters skulking in the dorms.

Alfie's Angels

Henriette Barkow, illustrated by Sarah Garson
Mantra Lingua, ISBN 1-85269-948-5 Vietnamese/English, £7.50 (pbk)

With quirky, cheerful Quentin Blake-like illustrations, this is the story of Alfie, who wants to be an angel in his school play even though this is a role customarily filled by a girl. Although dual-language, this book is set in a typical English-speaking classroom where the children paint pictures, play football, put on plays and learn music. There is considerable stereotypical characterisation of children, teachers and family, but nevertheless this could be a useful book for foreign-national children trying to adapt to life in an English-speaking community. There is plenty of opportunity for additional chat about the activities illustrated, while the dual text makes it more accessible for those struggling to learn English or for reading at home with non-English-speaking parents. This book is also available in English combined with Albanian, Arabic, Bengali, Chinese, Czech, Farsi, French, German, Gujarati, Italian, Panjabi, Portuguese, Polish, Russian, Serbo-Croat, Somali, Spanish, Tamil, Turkish or Urdu.

JMi

A Wild Elephant at Camp

Anupama Mohorkor, illustrated by Emanuele Scanziani
Tara Publishing, ISBN 81-86211-73-X, £5.25 (pbk)

This realistic story describes how Kutti, a young tribal boy, becomes the carer for an abandoned baby elephant found in the elephant sanctuary that is Kutti's home. How Ramu grows strong, bottle-fed on powdered milk, is described in matter-of-fact language. The human-like jealousy felt by an older elephant, Tulasi, overlooked in the fuss about Ramu's arrival, is highlighted. But it is Tulasi who comes to Ramu's rescue when he is stuck in strong currents in a river. The story is based on true incidents at a real elephant sanctuary in South India. There are several pages of photographs and description of life at the camp, and children who have enjoyed the story will be fascinated by these. The environmental need for sanctuaries like this one is discussed, as is the role of the mahouts who specialise in training and looking after elephants. An interesting book, which will appeal to those who are interested in facts as well as a good story.

VC

An t-Uan Beag Dubh

Elizabeth Shaw, arna aistriú ag Daire Mac Pháidín
Cló Uí Bhriain, ISBN 0-86278-867-6, €5.50 (clúdach bog/pbk)

This is an utterly charming book that would lend itself to a cosy reading session of pure delight, at home or at school. Young children will relate easily to the minimalist language and artwork and to the principal dramatis personae – the timid but resourceful little black sheep, the 'cocky' dog Póló, and the affectionate, diplomatic shepherd, with his strong survival instinct and impressive management skills, especially in the area of conflict resolution!

LÉARÁID Ó AN t-UAN BEAG DUBH

Leabhar beag gleoite é seo, scéilín simplí atá thar a bheith oiriúnach do leanaí óga. 'Múintear' cúpla ceacht luachmhar sa scéal – baintear siar as madra sotalach, faigheann 'an t-uan beag dubh' luach a shaothair agus éiríonn leis an aoire dícheallach cneasta fadhb éada (agus ealaíne!) a chur chun tairbhe dó féin agus dá thréad. Ní haon ionadh é gur aistríodh an scéal seo go Gearmáinis, go Spáinnis, go Danmhairgis, go Sualainnis, go Portaingéilis, go Laitvis, go Tuircis agus go Seapáinis freisin. Ba bhreá liom cóipeanna den leagan Gaeilge a fheiceáil i ngach aon leabharlann scoile agus i ngach aon leabharlann phoiblí.

J210,794 .

809
89282

UNíDh

A–Z and Back Again

written by children and parents, Derry and Sligo
Kids' Own Publishing Partnership, ISBN 1-902432-16-9, €10 (pbk)

The authors of this alphabet by children, for children, are drawn from both the settled and the Traveller community. The words chosen, the bold print designs illustrating them and the computer technology used to provide portraits of the contributors provide a  clear view of change in young society. Keys, kids, kites and a *katori* – the Urdu word for a small drinking bowl – jostle for space opposite lollipops and lugs (the Traveller word for ears), while M, of course, is for mobile phone and money, and W for waffles and 'wains' – a word for small children, common in Irish usage. The contributors' names appear alongside the relevant letters, as do excerpts from rhymes appropriate to the words. The composite nature of the group of authors is reflected in the riotous eclecticism of the illustrations and vocabulary alike. This book is a fundamental statement of the originality, flexibility and diversity of young twenty-first-century Ireland.

AP

Boots for a Bridesmaid

Verna Allette Wilkins, illustrated by Pamela Venus
Tamarind Press, ISBN 1-870516-30-3, £4.50 (pbk)

Nicky has been asked to be a bridesmaid at her Aunt Flora's wedding and reluctantly agrees. She doesn't like silly, ribbony dresses, doesn't want to carry flowers and hates satiny shoes. She likes cricket, and playing with her mates Jason and Rachid. Her mother tries to convince her that that it's a great honour to be asked to be a bridesmaid and, to placate her, allows her to wear boots instead of satin shoes, and even helps her to pick out a red pair. The girls in school tease Nicky when they find out she's wearing boots instead of shoes. However, all ends well – Nicky's aunt gets married, and Nicky gets a surprise on the day of the wedding. This is an uplifting book, and the illustrations, while slightly dated, are positive and dynamic. Commissioned by the Spinal Injury Association, Nicky's mum's disability – she is in a wheelchair – is subtly alluded to, but is not central to the story. Nicky isn't a particularly conventional girl, but she has lots of friends and a loving, supportive family, and is allowed to be who she wants to be.

MNíDh

Baba's Gift

Beverley and Maya Naidoo, illustrated by Karin Littlewood
Puffin, ISBN 0-670-91184-4, £10.99 (hbk)

'Lindi and Themba got up with the sun. Gogo was taking them to the sea for a day. "I have work to do," said Baba, "but I have made a present for you."' Baba makes a special boat for his grandchildren, Themba and Lindi. Their grandmother Gogo takes them to the sea, and they carry the boat with them, passing banana fields and sugar cane on the way. But when they forget about the boat and the sea claims it, the children are distraught. Luckily their Baba is an understanding man. A gentle story celebrating family and friends, with a rather twee ending, this is competently written, but it's the colourful illustrations by Karin Littlewood that really bring the characters and the African setting alive. Littlewood uses a glowing watercolour palette of greens, blues and reds, and her loose brushstrokes give a strong sense of movement and action. The faces of Lindi and Themba are full of character, and she captures their expressions perfectly.

SW

Brundibar

retold by Tony Kushner, illustrated by Maurice Sendak
Walker Books, ISBN 1-84428-028-4, £12.99 (hbk)

There are no new words to describe the genius of Maurice Sendak, whose artistry has made him one of the most significant figures in modern children's literature. Fatherless Pepicek and Aninku go to town to get milk for their sick mother, but they have no money. They decide to sing in the Town Square but are chased away by Brundibar, the hurdy-gurdy man. They meet a talking bird, cat and dog, who, along with three hundred and twenty children, help them. They sing and get lots of money, which Brundibar promptly steals. The townspeople turn on him, and the children get the milk to save their mother. Retold by Tony Kushner and presented in the form of a storyboard, using image, narrative and speech-bubbles, the book is based on the Czech children's opera *Brundibar*, by Hans Krása and Adolf Hoffmeister. Krása himself was murdered by the Nazis, as were many of those children forced to perform his opera in Terazin Concentration Camp. Already a winner of the New York Times Best Illustrated Books of 2004 award, this is a significant book relating to tyranny that needs to be included in any collection for children.

FO'S

Chopsticks

Jon Berkeley
Oxford University Press, ISBN 0-19-272456-8, £4.99 (pbk)

Set in a modern Hong Kong that is vividly evoked by detailed images, this is the story of a small mouse called Chopsticks who befriends one of the giant wooden dragons coiled around pillars at the entrance of a floating restaurant. The dragon confides that he would dearly love to fly away and see the world, but only the man who created and carved him, Old Fu, can release him from the pillar. Chopsticks visits Old Fu and learns the magic tune that will set the dragon free, and at the next full moon (and on each successive full moon) he and the dragon soar into the sky and fly away to see the world. Following each adventure, Chopsticks visits Old Fu to tell him of the wonders they have seen. The story unfolds, panel by panel, with a simple text accompanied by wonderfully vivid pictures, leaving the reader wanting more.

FO'S

Chuamar go léir ar Safáraí: ag taisteal is ag comhaireamh sa Tansáin

Laurie Krebs, arna mhaisiú ag Julia Cairns, arna aistriú ag Gabriel Rosenstock
An Gúm, ISBN 1-85791-480-5, €7.50 (clúdach bog/pbk)

This book shows us Tanzania's countryside and animals, through the eyes of ten young children who count the animals as they meet them on a walk. The Swahili word for each number appears alongside the numeral, allowing the reader to learn a few words of the language while simultaneously becoming acquainted with the country, the people, the animals and the numbers from one to ten. At the back, there is a most interesting brief account of the Masai, a map and some general information on Tanzania.

Nuair a leag mé mo shúil ar *Chuamar go léir ar Safáraí* den chéad uair, bhraitheas go raibh na hainmhithe go léir ag léim amach as na leathanaigh chugam. Bhainfeadh na pictiúir ildaite an radharc de do shúile. Tá an dearadh go han-mhaith agus an cló go breá mór, ionas gur furasta an téacs a léamh. Is é an file cumasach Gabriel Rosenstock a rinne an leagan Gaeilge, agus a rian sin ar cheol na cainte. Feictear an Tansáin trí shúile pháistí éagsúla sa tír agus iad ag comhaireamh na n-ainmhithe a fheiceann siad. Téann an léitheoir i dtaithí ar ainmneacha áille na bpáistí agus na n-ainmhithe. Déanann sé dearmad air go bhfuil sé ag foghlaim, tá an turas chomh taitneamhach sin.

CHUAMAR GO LÉIR AR SAFÁRAÍ

CNicA

Cleversticks

Bernard Ashley, illustrated by Derek Brazell
HarperCollins, ISBN 0-00-663855-4, £4.99 (pbk)

Ling Sung has just started school, but doesn't like it, as he doesn't seem to be able to do any of the things that the other children do. They can tie their laces, do up their coats or have a go at painting their names. Ling Sung much prefers helping his father to bathe his little sister or going swimming with his mother. It all changes at break-time, when his teacher notices him eating a broken biscuit using two paintbrushes as chopsticks. Everyone claps in admiration, and they all have a go — needless to say, without much success, but with a good deal of laughter. In the last pages, the children share their skills with one another. Any worry that children must be seen to be 'good at' something in order to be valued is subsumed in the message that we all learn things of value from our homes — something we need to remember as we encourage small children to benefit from and enjoy our primary schools.

LJ

Double the Love

Bernard Ashley, illustrated by Carol Thompson
Orchard Books, ISBN 1-84121-278, £4.99 (pbk)

This warm story celebrates grandparents and the valuable role they can play in children's lives. Blossom is lucky — she has two grandmothers: Nan and Gran. One lives in the city, the other in the country, and Blossom loves spending time with each. But she has never spent time with both together, until there is a party to celebrate the birth of Blossom's new baby brother. Blossom is delighted to see her two grandmothers together for the first time, and watches them getting to know each other. Nan has dark skin and wears wonderfully bright and patterned clothes, and Gran has pale skin and wears monotone colours. The two grandmothers share the joy of their grandchildren through music and dance, from 'Ring-a-ring-a-roses' to 'Tinga-Layo'. Carol Thompson's expressive watercolours, full of movement and fun, are a joy.

PO'D

Don't Cry Sly!

Henriette Barkow, illustrated by Richard Johnson
Mantra Lingua, ISBN 1-85269-652-4 Czech/English, £7.50 (pbk)

This is the dramatic tale of how a young fox called Sly, with the assistance of his new friend, Little Red the hen, succeeds in outsmarting his nagging mother. It is an engaging and humorous story in which the weak unite to outwit an oppressor; the written text is kept to a minimum and is appropriately simple yet pleasantly dramatic. The main attraction of this picture book lies in the illustrations. Warm, bright colours reflect the optimism central to this tale, and the absence of heavy borders creates a lightness of touch. The illustrations perfectly capture the personalities of each of the characters. Perspective is used effectively: when Sly is feeling small due to his mother's bullying, he is relegated to a small space, as if seen from a distance; his mother, in contrast, dominates the page. The central theme of an unlikely friendship between a fox and a hen will delight young readers from four to seven or eight years old. *Don't Cry Sly!* is available in twenty other dual-language editions: English with Albanian, Arabic, Bengali, Chinese, Farsi, French, German, Gujarati, Hindi, Italian, Panjabi, Polish, Portuguese, Serbo-Croat, Somali, Spanish, Tamil, Turkish, Urdu or Vietnamese.

ÁNicG

Fine Feathered Friend

Jamila Gavin, illustrated by Dan Williams
Egmont, ISBN 0-7497-4224-0, £3.99 (pbk)

Jamila Gavin's concise narrative follows the adventures of a young boy, Raju, who is reluctantly moved from the hustle and bustle of Bombay to spend a summer with his aunt and uncle in the Indian countryside. Raju soon realises that the farm has many more exciting experiences to offer than he originally anticipated. The story explores both the thrill of the big city and the appeal of the countryside, yet never

succumbs to stereotypical representations of India. In his illustrations, Williams uses similar shades and colours to represent both city and country life, drawing parallels between the two worlds, while the text documents their differences. The relevance of the narrative to issues of multiculturalism, acceptance and tolerance is not limited to the Indian characters and locale: as Raju opens his mind to new experiences, he realises the rewards he can reap from this. This is a well-told story that signals the benefits of diversity.

PW

Grandma Nana

Véronique Tadjo
Milet, ISBN 1-84059-285-0, £4.99 (pbk)

Bold-colour backgrounds, clever framing, bright patterning, faux-naïf paintings and collage techniques are the hallmarks of this book's visual appeal. This is less a story than a descriptive, evocative essay on Grandma Nana's relationship with children and her role in ensuring cultural continuity within the community. Grandma's perspective on the world is poetic: rain, she says, is the sun's tears; trucks don't knock down children – rather, they eat them up. Images convey a sense of a strong, affirming woman, at home with both the old and the modern civilisations that she straddles, telling riddles about aeroplanes and concocting herbal medicines. The book returns again and again to the doll that is always at Grandma's side, always represented as an icon rather than integrated into the fabric of the picture. Is the doll her soul, her alter ego, her guardian angel? No explanations are forthcoming, as is entirely proper. The final page hints at Grandma's approaching death without actually mentioning it. We are told that, with her doll on her lap, the very old woman watches the sun going down 'slowly, slowly,' for a very long time. The repetition of that word 'slowly' has the stuff of poetry in it. A lovely book.

MST

Hen-sparrow Turns Purple

Gita Wolf, illustrated by Pulak Biswas
Tara Publishing, ISBN 81-56211-19-5, £14.99 (accordion pages/scroll)

This book, already a Biennale of Illustrations Bratislava award-winner, is simply stunning. The whole format of the book captivates the reader: it is presented in landscape rather than portrait format, to open like a scroll. The accordion pages are hand-printed on handmade paper, and each page is presented with text to the left and image to the right. Each image recalls the exquisite art of Indian miniature-painting, and each illustration is bordered and set against a colour panel. It is breathtaking. The story is a cheery one: Hen-sparrow falls into a vat of purple dye, setting off a train of events that turns the whole kingdom upside down. Cock-sparrow plucks out his feathers on seeing his mate turned purple, the tree sheds her leaves, the buffalo breaks off his horns, the river turns salty and the peacock sheds his plumage. Even the king, queen and prince must deal with the fact that Hen-sparrow is now purple. Hen-sparrow remains untouched by all these reactions and decides that she quite likes being purple! An excellent book.

HEN-SPARROW TURNS PURPLE

FO'S

Jamaica Tag-Along

Juanita Havill, illustrated by Anne Sibley O'Brien
Egmont, ISBN 1-4052-0938-0, £4.99 (pbk)

This is one of a series of picture books about Jamaica, her family and her friends. *Tag-Along* features Ossie, her big brother, who doesn't want her present when he's playing football with his friends. Jamaica decides to allow a younger child to join in her game; *she* understands about being excluded. Many children know how it feels when you're not allowed to join in, and as a read-aloud book this offers an opportunity to talk about feelings and experiences. There are positive images of groups of children from diverse backgrounds playing together, as can be seen every day in cities and towns all over Europe, and a subtext about empathy. The characters have real personality, and the authentic images of ethnic difference lend reality to a story that is universal.

AO'D

Lima's Red Hot Chilli

David Mills, illustrated by Derek Brazell
Mantra Lingua, ISBN 1-85269-470-X Yoruba/English, £7.50 (pbk)

Hungry young Lima goes to the kitchen for a snack. She rejects the coconut, the samosas and the spaghetti, and the sweets are too high up. Finally she decides on the red-hot chilli her mother had warned her against. Her mouth on fire, she is offered water, ice-cream, jelly and mango by helpful relatives, but nothing works as well as the milk her grandmother gives her. She has learned her lesson and is no longer hungry. This is a simple story in a modern setting within an extended Indian family. The full-colour illustrations are warm and realistic, closely supporting the narrative. The experience of a child inadvertently eating very spicy food, and the resulting fuss and drama, will be common to most cultures. The book is unremarkable in itself but could be a treasure because it is available in big-book format and in so many dual-language versions: English with Albanian, Arabic, Bengali, Chinese, Farsi, French, Greek, Gujarati, Japanese, Khmer, Korean, Panjabi, Portuguese, Serbo-Croat, Somali, Tamil, Turkish, Urdu or Vietnamese.

IB

My Daddy is a Giant

Carl Norac, illustrated by Ingrid Godon
Mantra Lingua, ISBN 1-84444-525-9, Irish/English, £7.50 (pbk)

Dads are invincible, as if we didn't know! And this is especially true of the dad who features in this humorously illustrated book. A wonderful relationship between father and son, showing their natural bonds of love and friendship, bursts out from these pages. Each is filled with enormous pride in the other. The boy is awestruck by his father, hero and protector, while the father revels in a buddy-type friendship with his son.

Tá atmasféar iontach grámhar le braith sa leabhar: tá maolgháire, gráinteacht agus barróga mar chuid lárnach de na cluichí beaga simplí atá á n-imirt – folach bíog, cluichí liathróide, mirlíní, marcaíocht ar dhroim an athar agus eile. Amuigh faoin spéir is mó a bhíonn an spórt ar siúl, agus na gníomhaíochtaí éagsúla i dtiún le rithim na séasúr – duilleoga ag titim, éin ag tógáil a neadacha, laethanta geala gréine agus ar eile. Cuirfidh an leabhar seo gliondar ar léitheoirí óga! Aistríodh an leabhar seo go teanga is tríocha – Albáinis, Polainnis, Sínis, Spáinnis, Vietnaimis agus Yoruba ina measc.

AMK/UNiDh

Papa's Latkes

Michelle Edwards, illustrated by Stacey Schuett
Walker Books, ISBN 0-7636-0779-7, £10.99 (hbk)

Now that Dora and Selma's Mamma is dead, who will make the latkes for Chanukah? Can Papa really make them as well as Mamma used to? Dora and Selma are not convinced. *Papa's Latkes* is the moving story of a family that must find a way of coping with its loss and grief, at a time of year when not being with one's loved ones can be impossible to bear. Chanukah should be a time of celebration, but how can the family celebrate when the person who used to make the festivities happen is no longer there? Not all readers will be familiar with the Jewish festival of Chanukah, but the way in which information about Jewish holidays is interwoven with a universal theme immediately establishes common ground. There are no explanations of Jewish customs, but there is just enough information to make those unfamiliar with the Jewish way of life eager to learn more. The illustrations, executed in soft pastels and chalks, warmly convey the poignant sadness of the story, while the domestic interiors effortlessly bring Chanukah and the Jewish culture to life. Gentle and tender, this story weaves its magic without artifice or overt didactic intent, and the two girls with their ever-changing expressions and bright eyes are instantly likeable.

LMy

Princess Katrina and the Hair Charmer

Christina Shingler, illustrated by Derek Brazell
Tamarind Press, ISBN 1-870516-68-0, £6.99 (pbk)

To everyone else, Katrina is a perfect African princess. But Katrina wonders if a 'girl with hair like mine [can] really be a proper Princess?' Katrina has 'springy curls…that refused to lie flat'. Zuri, the Hair Charmer, is summoned by Fussfeathers, Katrina's pet parrot, and creates a variety of hairstyles for Katrina. Her self-confidence enhanced, Katrina returns to the palace feeling 'taller, prettier and happier'. On one level, this story has elements of the fairy tale, in that dreams do come true in unexpected ways; but it also subtly addresses the issue of self-image and the ideal of beauty as transmitted through the media. The illustrations are vivid, with lots of cerise-pinks, lime-greens and other strong colours that will appeal especially to young girls, and the language is full of imagery.

RH

The Boy on the Beach

Niki Daly
Bloomsbury, ISBN 0-7475-4684-3, £5.99 (pbk)

This is a wonderfully exuberant, funny and reassuring picture book. Niki Daly's watercolour illustrations are fluid and expressive and perfectly capture the child's character and the scene on the beach, which is probably somewhere in South Africa, but could be anywhere. We don't know the boy's name until the end, when a friendly lifeguard asks his name; in response, mouth full of ice-cream, he draws it in the sand with his toes. The exuberant illustrations are accompanied by a loosely rhyming text, which whisks along at a pace that is great fun to read aloud, and you can just feel the speed of the boy as he tears around the place, eventually getting lost in the sand dunes, only to be reunited with his parents by the lifeguard. This is a terrific book, one not to be missed. Niki Daly is the winner of two IBBY awards for illustration.

LJ

That's My Mum

Henriette Barkow, illustrated by Derek Brazell
Mantra Lingua, ISBN 1-85269-604-4, English/Serbo-Croat, £7.50 (pbk)

This story looks at the challenges facing those in mixed-race families where the children don't look like one or other of their parents. Charming and colourful illustrations complement the text, telling how Mia and her friend Kai overcome the difficulties they face in the school and in the playground when their friends mix up their mums. This book is perhaps most useful for a discussion or teaching session, rather than for independent readers, as the limited story-line may not hold the attention of young readers, but it could also be read and enjoyed at home with non-English-speaking parents. This is a dual-language book, also available in English combined with Albanian, Arabic, Bengali, Chinese, Czech, Farsi, French, German, Gujarati, Italian, Panjabi, Portuguese, Somali, Spanish, Turkish, Urdu or Vietnamese.

JMi

THAT'S MY MUM

The Bush

Bernard Ashley, illustrated by Lynne Willey
Tamarind Press, ISBN 1-870516-60-5, £5.50 (pbk)

This story, set in Africa, shows a family's attempt to earn a living by rearing rabbits. Young Joyce knows that the rabbits aren't pets, yet she becomes especially fond of one that she names Kipenzi. Her mother tells her that, when they're fully grown, the rabbits will go to the Bush; but to Joyce, this symbolises freedom and open space, and she is looking forward to the day when the rabbits will be released there. Unbeknownst to her, the Bush is a restaurant in the nearby city. The story is well written, with great symmetry and an unexpected ending, and keeps the reader in suspense. It could be read as a serial and could provide many opportunities for prediction and discussion. The illustrations are graphic, colourful and well linked to the story line.

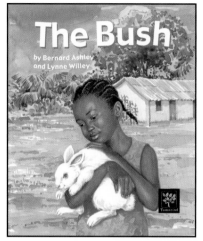

JMa

The Feather

Dot Cleeve, illustrated by Kim Harley
Tamarind Press, ISBN 1-870516-61-3, £5.50 (pbk)

Paula finds a feather by a river under a tree and asks all the birds she meets who owns it, but no one knows. Paula's feather is grey, but the kingfisher's feathers are blue, the wagtail's are yellow and the pheasant's are copper-brown. As Paula talks to the various birds, her feather collection grows as each bird offers her one of its feathers. The birds tell her to put the feathers up to her eye, and when she looks through the feathers, she sees different landscapes. The idea of seeing these different worlds, each of which corresponds to the colour of the feather involved, is a clever one. Quite why Paula sees a tropical beach through the kingfisher's feather is, however, hard to understand: surely a wooded river scene would have made more sense? Cleeve's choice not to make the worlds Paula sees reflect the actual habitats of the birds in question seems odd. *The Feather* is a book aimed directly at little girls, and Paula's bright stripy top, braided hair, pink runners and funky flowery hat are bound to make her a hit with young fashion-conscious readers. The multicoloured feather collection that Paula puts together at the end of this book stands as an effective metaphor for cultural diversity.

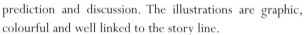

LMy

The Colour of Home

Mary Hoffman, illustrated by Karin Littlewood
Frances Lincoln, ISBN 0-7112-1991-5, £5.99 (pbk)

In a way that is engaging and sensitive, this book tells the story of Hassan and his family, who are making a new life in England after leaving their home in Somalia. When he lacks the words to talk about his family's journey to England, and the events that precipitated it, Hassan continues his story through the pictures he paints at school. Later, painting allows him to show his love for Somalia, while he gradually learns the words to express himself in a new language. Littlewood's vibrant watercolours perfectly capture the colours of Africa – colours that Hassan's family bring to England, and which serve as an eloquent metaphor,

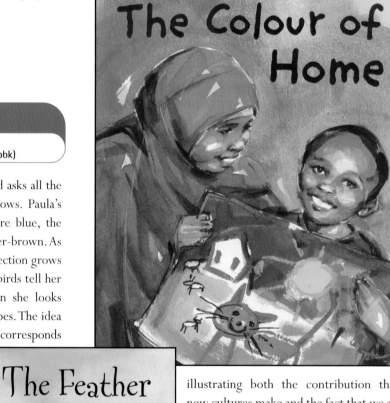

illustrating both the contribution that new cultures make and the fact that we all bring something of our old homes to our new ones. Without avoiding the reality of why people are sometimes forced to leave their homes, or providing a simplistic resolution to the challenges that Hassan faces in his new life, this story is ultimately a hopeful and profoundly uplifting one.

JFi

The Friday Nights of Nana

Amy Hest, illustrated by Claire A Nivola
Walker Books, ISBN 0-7445-9426-X, £4.99 (pbk)

Jennie and Nana, her grandmother, spend the day preparing for the Sabbath dinner. This gentle story is drawn forward only by Jennie's yearning for the time for the next of the clearly familiar activities to arrive. Amy Hest's simple but timeless text captures the loving relationship between the young girl and her grandmother. Much of the charm of the book, however, comes from the illustrations. Simple interiors in line and wash are enlivened by the selective use of strong colours; views framed in windows and open doors remind us of Dutch interiors; snow spins in Van Gogh-like swirls against the glass. Finally, 'it is the best time'; the family arrives and we, as privileged viewers, look in on their gathering through the window. This book will delight both Jewish and non-Jewish readers. It is enriching for the reader to see how Jennie and Nana are drawn together by the familiar activities of preparing for the Sabbath meal.

AF

Where's Jamela?

Niki Daly
Frances Lincoln, ISBN 1-84507-031-3, £10.99 (hbk)

When Jamela's mama gets a new job, the family – including Gogo, Jamela's granny – must move to a new house. Jamela is not happy with her mama's plans, as she knows she'll miss her old life and her school friends. A few days later, the family packs up their belongings, but during the move Jamela goes missing. Mama and Gogo are frantic and search the neighbourhood for the little girl – but there's a happy ending to the tale. This is a life-affirming story set in South Africa, with vibrant watercolour illustrations by the author, and a great book for reading aloud to slightly older children.

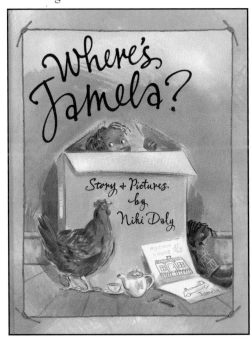

SW

The Song of the Trees

Kenneth Steven, illustrated by Lily Moon
Little Tiger Press, ISBN 1-85430-790-8, £9.99 (hbk)

A long time ago, before the first white man set foot in the New World, a little Indian girl dreamed something horrific. Lolita dreamed that great white birds were crossing the ocean, that the woods were shaking and all the trees were crying. Her father told her not to worry, but when one morning she saw great boats with white sails coming towards her on the sea, she was afraid. This is the story of how white colonisers chopped down native Indian forests in the name of progress. It is not, however, a story about destruction, but a positive story about the strength of the human spirit, for Lolita does not leave after the forest is destroyed, but stays and tries to put things right. The ending makes this book a particularly effective ecological story, as it does not lead the reader to despair but rather stresses the need for individual action. Moon's illustrations, with their subtle ethnic flair, beautifully evoke the Indian atmosphere. Particularly effective is her use of colour: when the people and animals are living happily in the forest, the illustrations are dominated by bright greens and yellows, while when Lolita is in the treeless desert, rich reds and purples form the base colours.

LMy

SUSAN GALLWEY AND BENI OBURU

Storyworlds

The Storyworlds project selects books with common themes to creatively discuss issues that arise in intercultural and development education.

STORYWORLDS, a joint project of Cultural Links and the Waterford One World Centre, grew out of a desire to encourage young children to think about everyday life in distant places. We were aware of the ways in which good stories could open up windows into other worlds. We also recognised that multicultural books could work against stereotypes and could help children to form positive images of different countries and cultures. The Storyworlds project was designed to explore the possibilities of using storybooks in the context of development education and intercultural education.

As the children became involved in the stories, they extended their knowledge of the world

Working with two groups of first- and second-class pupils, we designed a series of eight workshops based on storybooks and supported by creative and co-operative learning activities. To give structure to the project, we chose books that were linked by the theme of 'home', a need that all people in the world share.

After an introductory session on the idea of 'home', each of the next five workshops featured a story set in a different continent. We shared the story with the class and then worked as a group on a story-based activity focusing on homes. For example, when looking at Ann Grifalconi's *The Village of Round and Square Houses* (1989) – set in Cameroon – we dramatised the story-within-the-story, in which the grandmother recounts why the villagers live in two different types of houses.

In each session, the book provided the pathway into the distant community. Discussion of the book led the project participants to consider questions such as 'What would it feel like to live here?', 'What things are important to the people in the story?' and 'Are there connections between this place and our own community?'. In the two final workshops, we brought the project together by constructing 'dream houses'. These shoe-box creations combined imaginative input from the children with features of the homes we had studied in previous weeks.

Cultural Links and the Waterford One World Centre have also developed another section of the Storyworlds project, in which the theme of 'home' has been expanded to encompass the issues surrounding 'moving home'. This section features books about moving home, set in different countries, cultures and historical eras. It is designed to raise awareness of the migration of people and to explore how people feel about leaving their homes for new and unfamiliar places. It presents opportunities to explore a range of relevant issues in today's increasingly diverse primary classrooms. The work of the Cultural Links organisation, with its emphasis on how we are all enriched by new influences, forms a vital component of this new phase of the project.

All along, the project has been driven by the children's responses to the stories. As the children became involved in the stories, they extended their knowledge of the world. They became aware of a range of perspectives and they developed empathy with people from different backgrounds. Most importantly, they made connections between themselves and the wider world.

In each session, the book provided the pathway into the distant community

For those involved, the Storyworlds project has opened up some of the many possibilities for using multicultural storybooks to explore the world that we all share. We look forward to discovering where new books and new ideas may lead us.

Storyworlds was funded by the Development Education Unit of Development Cooperation Ireland.

SUGGESTED RESOURCES:
A Different Story. Tide DEC, 1999, 0948838582
Place in Storytime. Geographical Association, 1996, 0899085211
Storyworlds. Humanities Education Centre, 1996, 1873928580
Start with a Story. Supporting young children's exploration of issues. Tide DEC, 2002, 0948838795
Talking Drum. Christian Aid, 1996, 0904379246

BOOKS DISCUSSED IN THIS ARTICLE:
Grifalconi, Anne, *The Village of Round and Square Houses*. Macmillan, 1989, 0333485211*

SUSANNA COGHLAN

Dancing Roads

Learning English as a foreign language is becoming increasingly popular in Cambodia. Susanna Coghlan looks at some of the ways in which books can improve the teaching of the language, particularly in rural areas.

photo: Phillip Butler

MOST OF RURAL CAMBODIA suffers from a severe lack of basic infrastructure. While the country's tourist industry continues to grow, few travellers venture outside of the key destinations for foreign visitors. Off the tourist trail, the few roads that are sealed are badly maintained, and most are still dirt. Such roads are known locally as 'dancing roads' because of the way in which one is flung around when travelling along their rutted surfaces.

Still suffering from the legacy of Pol Pot and the Khmer Rouge, Cambodia has few publishing houses and there has been little development of a 'reading culture'. Adult female literacy is currently at sixty per cent. Seventy-five per cent of the population is engaged in subsistence farming.

In most public schools, books are a scarce resource. The Cambodian Ministry for Youth and Sport is, however, currently working towards the installation of libraries in rural schools. One NGO, Room to Read, has built libraries and computer labs in schools in some of the country's most deprived areas, stocking them with English and Khmer-language children's books. Room to Read's mandate also includes supporting the publication of children's books in indigenous languages and providing long-term scholarships for girls.

Books are an important resource for teachers and students alike. Reading to the children can be a welcome break from classroom drills and unexciting textbooks, and allows students time in which to listen to and absorb language and information. This practice can lead to spontaneous classroom discussions and can break down the customary formality of teacher-pupil interaction in Cambodian schools. It also provides opportunities for students to voice their own opinions and ideas so that they become truly engaged in the learning process.

Although English is taught in many schools throughout Cambodia, most young students in rural areas will rarely encounter the spoken or written language in any aspect of their daily lives. Often even the teachers themselves have had very few opportunities to experience the English language outside of the classroom.

The desire to read English-language books can offer children living in rural Cambodia an incentive to learn English. Using 'real' books in the classroom allows the children to experience the language in a new way, outside of the textbooks and the largely rote-based learning system. Using 'real books' allows for means of self-expression, discussion and creativity.

For the many children who live in isolated villages along Cambodia's dancing roads, the creation of libraries and reading spaces will have an effect beyond that of language development alone. The availability of a wide range of books in schools can form a vital link with the world outside their community – providing insight into new places, people, customs and concepts, increasing children's understanding of the wider world and igniting their curiosity.

Creating libraries in schools will help to establish the importance of books and reading in children's lives – fostering the ability for independent learning and research – and providing a place where children explore and enjoy the pleasure of books at their own pace.

In a country where it is estimated that almost a quarter of the child population is working full-time, access to books, for pleasure and for learning, brings the potential for growth and change.

An Sealgaire agus an Crann Éabainn

Nelda La Teef, arna aistriú ag Úna Ní Chonchúir
An Gúm, ISBN 1-85791-552-6, €7.50 (clúdach bog/pbk)

Here is a sunburst of luxuriant vegetation, radiant colours and exotic fabrics, all presented in the context of a resourceful hunter's determination to solve a problem of romance. He enlists the help of a woodpecker, a spider and a butterfly in his effort to pierce a specific ebony tree with his arrow and win himself a beautiful and shrewd wife. The book is a veritable feast for the senses – the eyes revel in a riot of colour and shape, the ears in the readily imagined environmental music and flower-scents, while the touch appreciates the sensuous, rippling fabrics.

Seoid chríochnaithe é an leabhar seo – athinsint ar scéal béaloidis a thugann léargas don léitheoir ar ghnéithe de chultúr na hAfraice. Tuigeann an sealgaire seiftiúil fírinne an tseanrá 'i dteannta a chéile is fearr iad' agus is le cabhair na gcarad a éiríonn leis sa triail a chaitheann sé a sheasamh chun cailín óg álainn a bhuachaint mar bhean chéile dó féin. Idir líofacht an aistriúcháin, leagan amach is cruinneas an téacsa, agus tarraingteacht an chlúdaigh, is mór an chreidiúint don fhoilsitheoir an leabhar breá seo.

UNíDh

Bambert's Book of Missing Stories

Reinhart Jung, translated by Anthea Bell, illustrated by Peter Allen
Egmont, ISBN 0-7497-4705-6, £4.99 (pbk)

Finding it painful to walk, Bambert relies on Mr Bloom, the grocer downstairs, for food, drink and occasional company. With more than a thousand books in his library, he sees the world through the eyes of poets and writers. He holds conversations with the moon, which seems to know as many stories as he does, and he writes these down in his Book of Wishes. With space in his book for only one more story, Bambert decides to tear the book into separate parts and send each, attached to a tissue-paper hot-air balloon powered by tea-lights, to find its own setting. He also sends four blank sheets of paper and secretly hopes the last story will write itself. Months pass before one of the stories returns to him, in a letter from Ireland, and immediately it seems to him that Ireland must always have been the story's setting. Gradually, the stories return, now with settings from all around the world: one tells of a child's kindness, another reveals the power of truth, one is very British in its black humour, another

a tragic account of the horrors of the war in Sarajevo. And when Bambert dies trying to rescue the four blank sheets that were caught on his roof, his friend Mr Bloom writes the eleventh story: that of Bambert's arrival on the 'far side of the dream', where he has been reunited with his characters. A very special book: unsentimental, truthful and extremely powerful.

LM

Benjy's Ghost

Jacqueline Roy
Walker Books, ISBN 0-7445-9078-7, £4.99 (pbk)

The way in which Benjy's father breaks the news that he is to marry again could serve as a textbook example of how not to make such an announcement. Benjy's understandable refusal to cooperate causes domestic disharmony and discord, until eventually he becomes reconciled to the fact that his new family may be a 'proper' one after all. Jonah the dog plays an unusual and unorthodox role in helping Benjy to reach this conclusion and come to terms with both his situation and himself, and this provides the main area of interest in this otherwise predictable and pedestrian tale. The adult characterisation is stereotyped and one-dimensional, and as a result both Benjy's father and his new stepmother – and hence the new family set-up – lack credibility, undermining the reader's belief in the story. It is significant that the one character who is allowed to speak with an individual voice, seven-year-old Kalya, comes across as a lively young person who engages our interest and attention. Short sentences and routine vocabulary may make this book attractive to hesitant readers.

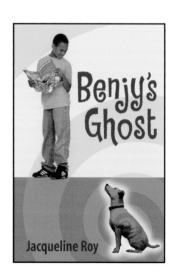

JF

LÉARÁID Ó EACHTRA I GCAIREO

Eachtra i gCaireo

Isobel Ní Riain, arna mhaisiú ag Elizabeth Stoll
An Gúm, ISBN 1-85791-463-5, €5.25 (clúdach bog /pbk)

Eachtra i gCaireo is a simple illustrated story of two Egyptian children, Ahmed and Heba, who visit the market area of Khan El Khalili and encounter Laura, a lost American girl. This is an informative book, particularly in relation to Muslim culture and lifestyle. A central theme is inequality due to class and gender: the female orphan Heba will never have the same educational and social opportunities as her male friend, Ahmed. The reality of such inequality creates an unsettling, albeit realistic, backdrop to the story. The dependence on money from foreigners, mainly Americans, also creates a rather sour aftertaste for both the reader and Ahmed.

Tá roinnt mhaith steiréaphlátaí sa leabhar seo: go háirithe an nasc a dhéantar idir Meiriceá agus saibhreas, idir an Éigipt agus bochtaineacht. De réir an leabhair seo, is ag na fir amháin a bhíonn seans ar dhul chun cinn sa saol san Éigipt!

ÁNicG

Esperanza Rising

Pam Munoz Ryan
The Chicken House, ISBN 1-903-43498-X, £5.99 (pbk)

Esperanza is the spoiled and petted daughter of a wealthy vineyard owner in 1920s Mexico, with nothing more to worry about than the number of presents she will receive for her thirteenth birthday. But her carefree life is shattered when her beloved father is murdered by bandits and her greedy uncles take over the vineyard. Forced to flee from their home, Esperanza and her mother begin a new life in California. Picking fruit and living in a tiny cabin, which they share with another family, is a far cry from their privileged existence in Mexico; but Esperanza soon learns to deal with the challenges she faces, and comes to value the bonds of family and friendship above all else. Based on the true story of the author's grandmother, *Esperanza Rising* gives a vivid insight into the experience of Mexican immigrants in the United States. Issues of prejudice, discrimination and hardship are brought to the fore through the eyes of the teenage heroine. The story is beautifully written, and readers will sympathise with the strong character of Esperanza as she reaches a new maturity and lives up to her name – the Spanish word for hope.

ESPERANZA RISING

NMac a'B

Eye of the Wolf

Daniel Pennac, translated by Sarah Adams, illustrated by Max Grafe
Walker Books, ISBN 0-7445-9010-8, £4.99 (pbk)

A truly original story about friendship, this is the memorable tale of a wolf from the Far North and a boy from Africa, who 'with all the time in the world' gradually reveal to each other the troubles and hardships they have experienced, worlds apart. The wolf has only one eye, because he lost it years earlier, when he was captured and brought to the zoo. The boy has two eyes, but closes one and discovers in the wolf's eye what nobody has ever seen before: in the iris, the boy reads the story of Blue Wolf, his sister Shiny Straw and the dangers of hunters in the silent snows of Alaska. The story finishes, and the boy sees his own image appear in the wolf's eye: he has become the wolf's most recent memory. In return, he allows the wolf to share his memories, and with Blue Wolf we read of Africa N'Bia, the young boy who accompanies camel-trader Toa across the continent, gathering stories of the three Africas and learning to tell these at night round the fires. Winner of the Marsh Award for Children's Literature in Translation, this is a magical tale that will be enjoyed by readers of all ages, on many different levels.

EYE of the WOLF
DANIEL PENNAC
illustrated by Max Grafe

LM

Flying with Icarus and Other Stories

Curdella Forbes
Walker Books, ISBN 0-7445-9067-1, £4.99 (pbk)

The heat of the Caribbean landscape shimmers behind these seven stories. The writing is clear, vivid and imaginative and the voices of the individual characters are immediately convincing, to this non-Caribbean reader, at any rate. Adults are realistically drawn, sometimes warm-hearted and loving and sometimes narrow-minded and judgmental, providing a very convincing framework within which their children struggle to make sense of, and come to terms with, the daily events that affect them. As children do everywhere, they find their own solutions. A new boy unexpectedly stands up to the class bully, a little girl learns more than she realises by caring for a hurt seagull, and a child who is sent to boarding school copes with loneliness by holding to her ear a seashell 'with worlds inside'. Finally, a little boy who is 'medium and ordinary' learns through the magic of storybooks how to release the inner qualities that make him special. These stories are lively, varied, subtle and interesting. They are about discovery and growth – common enough themes, but the exotic setting and the imaginative use of language give them a special quality that lingers in the memory.

JF

Hurricane

Verna Allette Wilkins, illustrated by Tim Clarey
Tamarind Press, ISBN 1-870516-66-4, £5.99 (pbk)

The increasing incidence of natural disasters, and their devastating effects on our world, makes this publication particularly relevant. Troy and Nita live on a Caribbean island. When their school day is interrupted by a storm warning, the children are instructed to return home immediately; but, not realising the serious nature of the warning, they decide to visit a friend on the way. This delay means they have to battle their way through an increasingly fierce and terrifying storm. When they eventually reach the safety of home, more traumatic events follow as a tree smashes through the front of their house. The grandmother later tells stories of previous storms to entertain the people who gather in the house, allowing the reader to realise that storms have come and gone before and that, though there is loss of life and devastation, life always returns to normal. The incidents are told realistically, at a fast-moving pace. Throughout the book, the illustrations, both colour and monochrome, complement and enhance this well-told story.

JD

Going North

Janice N Harrington, illustrated by Jerome Lagarrigue
Melanie Kroupa Books, Farrer Straus and Giroux,
ISBN 0-374-32681-9, $16 (hbk)

This is the first children's book by a very highly regarded storyteller, and her art can be heard in every rhythmic line. It tells the very moving story of African-American Jessie and her family, who leave their home in Alabama in the 1960s and head for Lincoln, Nebraska, where they hope to escape from the segregation and racism of the South and find a better life. The pain of leaving home and of parting from a beloved grandmother is poignantly conveyed in Jessie's words: 'I slip off my shoes and push my feet / Into the rusty sand. I wish my toes were roots. / I'd grow into a pin oak and never go away. / Would they let me stay if I were a tree?' When the family car begins to run out of petrol on the journey, the challenge of finding a petrol station that is not reserved for white people brings the horror of racial segregation to life in the most simple and effective way possible. There is restraint and economy at every point. The closing words are, 'Be brave. We're together. Pioneers.' Harrington redeems, with much grace, the American pioneer myth from its almost exclusively white and usually right-wing context, and reclaims it for African-Americans. The book has obvious relevance in today's Ireland, where many of our new immigrants are just such pioneers. It is beautifully illustrated in a painterly way, inspired by the Impressionists and perhaps by Edward Hopper, that conveys the warm haziness of the landscape and the confusion of feelings and impressions.

CK

Iqbal

Francesco D'Adamo, translated by Ann Leonori
Simon & Schuster, ISBN 0-689-83768-2, £7.99 (pbk)

This is not a biography; rather it is a novel based on the true story of Iqbal Masih's short life. Iqbal became a bonded labourer in the Pakistani carpet sheds at the age of six. At ten, he ran away and subsequently became a spokesperson for the Bonded Labour Liberation Front. For the next two years, he toured the world speaking out against the carpet industry. At twelve he was murdered – by, many suspect, those with a vested interest in that industry. His death was raised in the American Congress and in most European parliaments. Narrated by Fatima, a fictional child-weaver in the last factory where Iqbal worked, this book paints a very real picture of the brutal, degrading exploitation that is life for the 'almost six million children [who] are working in conditions of "forced and bonded labour"', as the introduction says. But this book is more than a retelling of the facts. It is a good starting point

for further investigation of the topic, and could be read in conjunction with Jamila Gavin's short story 'The Paradise Carpet' in *From Out of the Shadows* (reviewed in the 12+ section).

LO'L

Journey to Jo'burg

Beverley Naidoo
HarperCollins, ISBN 0-00-675455-4, £4.99 (pbk)

When their baby sister Dineo becomes sick, Naledi and Tiro decide to make a three-hundred-kilometre journey to fetch their mother, who is working as a maid in

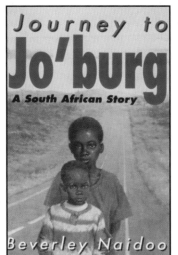

Johannesburg. Confronted by differences between city and country life and between older and younger generations, Naledi considers and questions her own position in South African society. Told in a clear, flowing style, this novel introduces complex issues and questions to young readers without over-simplification or condescension. Set in the time of apartheid, it examines everyday institutionalised prejudice – be it on the bus or at school – and shows that 'politics' touch children's lives at every level, giving readers the opportunity to ask questions about their own societies and cultures. Naledi and all the most important adult characters are female, a fact that might make the book less attractive to younger male readers; however, the children are helped along their journey by male figures, and one exiled, politically active brother is shown as a source of great pride to his family in Soweto. This is beautifully written, with a seemingly simple style that has a poetic clarity and intensity.

NM

Just Joshua

Jan Michael
The O'Brien Press, ISBN 0-86278-818-8, €8.95 (pbk)

This is a story about being different and about a child's search for identity. The 'mountain people' live 'at least one day's walk' above Joshua's small tropical coastal village, and

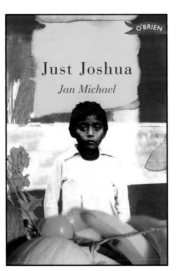

they are disliked and distrusted by the villagers. Joshua gradually realises that his father, a butcher and wood-carver, is a 'mountain man', and that he is different and, in the words of another orphan, 'not really one of us. He carves'. After the unexpected death of his father, Joshua is poised between two societies and feels he truly belongs to neither. He grasps at the chance of being adopted by a foreign couple because, with them, his past would no longer matter. In the end Joshua is able to find pride in his heritage and essential self and proclaims proudly that he is 'just Joshua'.

RH

Lionboy / Lionboy: The Chase

Zizou Corder
Puffin Books, ISBN 0-141-31726-4, £4.99 (pbk)
Puffin Books, ISBN 0-141-31756-6, £4.99 (pbk)

These books begin the story of Charlie Ashanti, whose mother is English and whose father is Ghanaian. Set in some future time when the natural resources of the earth have been depleted, the book offers a running commentary on the environment, the captivity of wild animals and the troubled issue of cloning. There is also suspense, fantasy and comedy in equal amounts, not to mention Charlie's asides on racism and prejudice as he experiences these. However, Charlie's real claim to fame is that he can speak 'cat'. Therefore, he can communicate with felines of every ilk, including lions. As he spends time with a floating circus, takes an utterly surreal journey through Europe on a private train and has a strange stay in a palace in Venice, there is the feeling that everything but the kitchen sink has gone into these books. That said, however, they have a strange charm that finally draws readers in and will leave them waiting for the final part of the trilogy.

JO'H

The Blood Stone

Jamila Gavin
Egmont, ISBN 1-4052-1284-5, £5.99 (pbk)

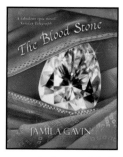

Based on a real character, Geronimo Veroneo, who travelled from Venice to India, this is an adventure story that is difficult to categorise: it is part thriller, part quest, part historical drama, full of magic and mystery – a story of epic scope that takes the reader halfway around the world. It begins in fifteenth-century Venice, where we are introduced to the Veroneo family. The father, a jeweller, goes to Hindustan in search of adventure, leaving his family in the care of a son-in-law who proves not to be the benign carer he was thought to be. Twelve years later, on hearing that his father is being held captive, the youngest son, Filippo, runs away to find him, taking with him as ransom a precious piece of jewellery called the Ocean of the Moon, said to have inspired the design of the Taj Mahal. The story moves from the labyrinthine canals and alleys of Venice across perilous stormy seas to Crete, through a sand storm in the scorching desert of Arabia, to India and the court of the Moghul Emperor Shah Jehan. This is a powerful, atmospheric story about good and evil, self-belief and hope, and is a particularly satisfying read for anyone interested in travel and other cultures.

PO'D

Spilled Water

Sally Grindley
Bloomsbury, ISBN 0-7475-6416-7, £10.99 (hbk)

Set in contemporary China, this appealing book tells of Lu Si-yan, who is eleven when sold into domestic service by her uncle. He believes that her life is a waste, like the spilled water of the title, and that her widowed mother and baby brother would be better off without her. In first-person narrative, the story follows little Lu Si-yan's struggle to return home, hampered by her own childish naïveté and the manipulative characters she meets. The poor rural communities relying on age-old traditional ways and the polluted industrial cities, with their bright lights and brash, exploitative lifestyles, are powerfully contrasted. Traditional Chinese imagery is used throughout, and absorbing references are made to daily life in China, although more detail would enrich the novel further. The language is simple and there is some lovely phrasing, but ultimately, the rather rushed ending and unexpected resolution left me disappointed, both for myself and for the characters.

JMi

The Reluctant Rajput

Richard Moverley, illustrated by David Dean
Egmont, ISBN 1-4052-1894-0, £3.99 (pbk)

Set in Nantapur village in Andhra Pradesh in Southern India, *Reluctant Rajput* explores another culture, detailing school, village and home life, food, dress, customs and religious practices. At school, Bhupinder and his classmates learn about the big cities of India, and their teacher tells them a story about a fort in  Rajasthan and about the Rajputs, a warrior caste, who built the forts and fought against the Moghul Empire. Bhupinder and his friends enjoy playing Rajputs and Moghuls after school, though the children of Nantapur do not have access to running water or electricity, making life difficult and labour-intensive. When Bhupinder's home chores are done, he falls asleep and has a vivid dream about a Moghul attack on the fort of Mherengarh. This overtly didactic story will open the eyes of any Western child to another culture's life and traditions. It will have special appeal to those children who are fond of battles and fierce warriors.

PO'D

The Rock Boy

Jan Michael
The O'Brien Press, ISBN 0-86278-721-1, €6.95 (pbk)

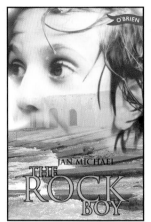

The author weaves fascinating details about Malta and its lifestyle, its unusual foods, its complex language and the homes of the islanders into this adventure full of action and excitement. Artan, the Rock Boy of the title, doesn't make an appearance until over a third of the way into the book, leaving the reader somewhat impatient for the 'real' story to start. The main character, Josephine, is interesting and well developed – independent and headstrong – but even with these qualities, her decision to keep secret the discovery of the badly injured Artan is somewhat far-fetched. Josephine's prosaic Dutch friend, Andreas, doesn't have quite the same strength of character but is a useful catalyst in the book. Although one or two plot elements seem to be left somewhat unresolved, this exciting tale will hold the attention of most young readers.

JMi

Travellers of the World: A Collection of Stories about Travelling

children in Drogheda and Dundalk, County Louth, Ireland
Kids' Own Publishing Partnership, ISBN 1-902432-21-5, €10 (pbk)

This anthology of journeys, both actual and aspirational, explores the idea of journeys with a number of Drogheda and Dundalk children, aged between seven and twelve, from all backgrounds: South African, Lithuanian, settled, Traveller, Pakistani. The authors tell of actual journeys of

immigration, on vacation, to family celebrations in locations from nearby Bettystown to Lithuania; of aspirational journeys as diverse as a balloon race across Pakistan, a trip to McDonalds and a voyage to meet angels in heaven. The typesetting varies idiosyncratically from tale to tale, and the photomontage accompanying each page supports the notion of diversity further by juxtaposing maps, photographs, abstract design or compilations of all three. This is an accessible, evocative and provocative celebration of the juxtaposition of experience and creative possibility, drawing on centuries-old and newly experienced cultural diversity in Ireland.

AP

Under the Spell of the Moon: Art for Children from the World's Great Illustrators

edited by Patricia Aldana
Groundwood Books, ISBN 0-88899-559-8, $25.00 (hbk)

Thirty-two entrancing double spreads show off the work of illustrators from nearly as many countries. Each artist has chosen a poem, rhyme, riddle, or short text to illustrate. Their styles vary greatly, from the abstract and surreal to more realistic interpretations of the chosen words – which, if they were originally written in any language other than English, are printed in the original with an English translation. This makes for a glorious feast of language and image from Japan, Iran, Argentina, Spain, Russia, China, Mali and many other countries. The names of some artists are familiar – Quentin Blake, Anthony Browne, Marie-Louise Gay, Peter Sís and Lisbeth Zwerger; others, like Pulak Biswas from India and Angela Lago from Brazil, are likely to be less well known, making this a treasure trove of exciting discoveries. At the back are biographies of the illustrators, all distinguished people, many winners of the Hans Christian Andersen Award. And my own favourite? It has to be Józef Wilkon's soft, brush-stroked little grey cat on a fence against a background of white.

VC

ILLUSTRATION FROM UNDER THE SPELL OF THE MOON

Did Charles Dickens Write Anything Other than *Oliver Twist, Sir?*

Ireland's Traveller community has a strong oral tradition. Teresa McGann relates some of her experiences of teaching reading to Traveller children and choosing books for the classroom.

ALTHOUGH LEARNING TO READ did not come easily to me, from my earliest years I have always had a passion for books. As a primary teacher working in a disadvantaged area, I brought my enthusiasm for books to my classroom where I built up a collection of colourful, well-written books for children.

Soon I recognised that not all books written about Travellers necessarily enhanced their reading skills

In 1992, I became involved in the teaching of Traveller children. I quickly realised that well-stocked class and school libraries were the key to enhancing the potential of Traveller children, who come from a strong oral tradition.

Initially, I sought out books about Travellers and their culture. Soon I recognised that, while these acknowledged and valued the children's background, not all books written about Travellers necessarily enhanced their reading skills. Consequently, I sought out well-written books in varying genres, rich in language, with strong storylines and appealing illustrations.

When selecting books, I tried to keep in mind age-appropriateness, the children's reading ability, their interests and their previous experience. Theme and plot were also considerations. Quality, rather than quantity, became the key.

Introducing authors and illustrators to the children fuelled their imaginations and their interest in the books they were reading. Children's Books Ireland (CBI) afforded me opportunities to meet living authors and illustrators. On one occasion, Marita Conlon-McKenna visited a local bookshop shortly after our class had read and reviewed her book *The Blue Horse* (1993), based on the life of a twelve-year-old Traveller girl living in Dublin. Marita asked one Traveller child, Kathleen, whether she thought the story of

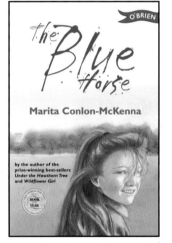

The Blue Horse was accurate. Kathleen confirmed that it was, and both she and Marita left the bookshop feeling satisfied with their work!

Teachers' expectations of their students are vital. I remember one instance when a teacher who had been on yard duty recalled laughingly to the staff how an eleven-year-old Traveller child had come to him and asked, 'Did Charles Dickens write anything else other than *Oliver Twist*, sir?' I responded by asking the teacher whether or not he had answered the child's question. Kathleen, who had just finished reading the book, lived in a roadside camp with few facilities. Even after she left school, she wrote regularly seeking books to read. She always included a review of the last book she had read.

On another occasion, Kevin, a young Traveller with reading difficulties, was in a learning support group. A visitor came in and asked him what his favourite book was.

'*Macbeth*,' replied Kevin, 'written by a fella called Shakespeare.'

On further questioning Kevin explained that he loved the play's themes – strong family bonds and conflict. His class teacher had been using an adapted version of the play with him.

Teachers' expectations of their students are vital

I believe that it is the job of the teacher to work with the children in his or her care and to seek out books of interest to them. With careful research, and using collective wisdom, you should be able to create a collection that will excite and entertain all your readers.

BOOKS DISCUSSED IN THIS ARTICLE:
Conlon-McKenna, Marita, *The Blue Horse*. The O'Brien Press, 1993, 0862783054

ARTICLE: DID CHARLES DICKENS WRITE ANYTHING OTHER THAN OLIVER TWIST, SIR?

38

NATHALIE BEAU TRANSLATED BY GEARÓID CRONIN

La Joie par les Livres, France

Nathalie Beau describes the diverse activities of La Joie par les Livres in promoting national and international children's books to audiences in France. The organisation also develops links between publishers in France, the Caribbean and Africa.

SINCE IT WAS ESTABLISHED IN 1965, La Joie par les Livres, which later became the Centre National du Livre pour Enfants (National Book Centre for Children), has attached particular importance to promoting awareness of other cultures through children's books.

Its founder, Geneviève Patte, who also founded IBBY France, established one of the very first children's libraries in France; and in the 1980s, this library was the forum in which the diverse activities of La Joie par les Livres gradually developed.

The international division of La Joie par les Livres advocates the inclusion of foreign-language books in libraries and schools

La Joie par les Livres (or the Centre National du Livre pour Enfants) is now linked to the French Ministry of Culture. It has an active publishing programme producing pedagogical aids, textbooks, essays, bibliographies and selections of foreign-language books. The journal *La Revue des Livres pour Enfants*, published six times yearly, presents a critical overview of new developments in publishing in France, with information and articles on young people's books and reading. *Takam Tikou*, an annual magazine dedicated to young people's literature and reading in Africa, the Arab world and the Caribbean, contains information about the publishing scene in these countries, book reviews and articles.

Ideally, schools and libraries should stock books written in the languages spoken by families in their community

The international division produces a specialised list of titles from these countries, organises an exchange network between professionals in the book trade and promotes links between organisations involved in children's books around the world. Every year a country is invited to represent its publishing scene at the Salon du Livre in Paris. La Joie par les Livres ensures that books for young people are included in the scope of these events, and authors and illustrators attend. To accompany this event, we publish a special issue of the *Revue des Livres pour Enfants*, in which we try to provide information on all aspects of children's books in the country in question. During the salon, IBBY France organises a day of meetings and debates encouraging a dynamic approach towards the discovery of new books.

IBBY France strives to promote French children's books abroad and campaigns for the recognition of foreign books in France. It has published four volumes dedicated to young people's books in Arabic, German, Spanish and English respectively. The Arabic volume was produced in collaboration with the Institut du Monde Arabe in Paris and German volume with the Goethe Institute in Nancy. Libraries and bookshops use these publications to guide them as they build up their stock.

The international division of La Joie par les Livres advocates the inclusion of foreign-language books in libraries and schools. These books are an important means of integrating immigrant communities. For children whose mother tongue is not the same as the language spoken in school, achieving competence in their own language is generally recognised as an aid to learning the language of the host country. Ideally, schools and libraries should stock books written in the languages spoken by families in their community.

There are many North African and Arab people living in France. Books in French dealing with the African and Arab cultural worlds must be developed, to enable children to learn the French language in a familiar context.

We currently have three exhibitions that are hired out to libraries, giving them the opportunity to promote and publicise books originating in other countries. 'Amabhuku: Thirty-Four African Illustrators' is an exhibition of posters introducing the illustrators and their works. 'African Books for Young People' comprises four hundred and fifty books from and about Africa. 'Kan ya ma kan' features a selection of one hundred French, Arabic and bilingual titles, maps and information about Arabic countries, a history of the region's literature for young people and presentations of two major texts: *Kalila and Dimna* and *The Arabian Nights*.

In collaboration with the French Department of Foreign Affairs, our intercultural department offers aid to African publishers for the publication and distribution of books for young people

As well as developing awareness of different cultures, foreign-language books provide children with an opportunity to heighten their understanding of languages in a fun and meaningful way.

La Joie par les Livres also provides professional development for those working in the area of children's books. Every year we organise a two-day training course to consider how we can increase the availability of foreign language books in libraries.

In collaboration with the French Department of Foreign Affairs, our intercultural department offers aid to African publishers for the publication and distribution of books for young people. This aid takes the form of an invitation to tender to African publishers, who send us the outlines of

Since it was established, 'La Joie par les Livres' has made children's books from all over the world available to children in France

their projects. A board of specialists chooses the best projects and puts forward suggestions for improvements. The Ministry undertakes to buy half of the print run, eliminating financial risks for the publisher. This has facilitated the publication of many books.

This initiative is a component of a global project aiming to support the whole spectrum of young people's books and reading in Africa – to foster creativity through writing or illustration workshops; to develop publishing and distribution by training booksellers; and to provide training for librarians.

Since it was established, La Joie par les Livres has made children's books from all over the world available to children in France. Our resource centre contains an international range of titles including reference works, magazines and specialist documentation. We are continuing to expand this range and to make a large number of foreign books available to readers, either in our resource centre or online. We intend to offer the entire range of children's books published in French-speaking Africa, as well as the best books produced in Europe, the Americas, the Arab world and Japan.

Across the Nightingale Floor

Lian Hearn
Young Picador, ISBN 0-330-49334-5, £6.99 (pbk)

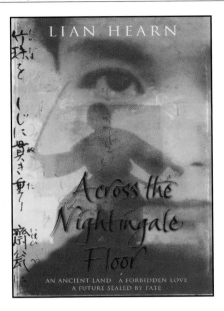

An epic tale of love, treachery and revenge set in a feudal Japanese society where nothing is as it seems. When Iida Sadamu and his Tohan warriors attack his remote mountain village, Tomasu is rescued by Shigeru, Lord Otori, sworn enemy of Lord Iida. Formally adopted by Shigeru and now a member of one of Japan's ancient dynasties, Tomasu, renamed Takeo, struggles to forget his former life and his deeply spiritual upbringing among the Hidden people. He gradually learns that he is by birth a member of the Tribe, warriors with supernatural skills and prior claim to his loyalties. When he falls in love with Kaede, betrothed to Shigeru on the instructions of the Tohan lord, formal and rigid codes of honour and loyalties are tested to the limit. Set in a mythical world whose impenetrable forests, flat plains bright with rice fields, and deep mountain passes are vividly and exquisitely described, this is the atmospheric and engrossing first book in a trilogy, reviewed in this section.

LM

A Little Piece of Ground

Elizabeth Laird
Macmillan, ISBN 0-330-43743-7, £4.99 (pbk)

This is an unashamedly one-sided account of what it is to be a Palestinian teenager in the occupied territories of Ramullah. The frustrations, political tensions, prejudices and family heartbreaks are brilliantly evoked from the first-person point of view of the protagonist, Karim Aboudi. The novel stands alongside *The Bookseller of Kabul* or *The Diary of Anne Frank* in its searing literary honesty, not seeking to answer any political question but simply telling it how it is from a particular perspective. Giving the reader access to a teenage culture similar to his or her own with its accounts of school, love, family and cultural tension, the book brings into sharp relief how such commonplace experiences buckle under the superimposition of an occupying force, and shows how a single shift in circumstance transforms universal quotidian preoccupations. Tersely and sensitively written, this is a ruthlessly passionate account.

AP

A Single Shard

Linda Sue Park
Oxford University Press, ISBN 0-19-271958-0, £4.99 (pbk)

A charming and delightful tale set in late twelfth-century Korea, this is the story of twelve-year-old Tree-ear, who lives under the village bridge, cared for by his old friend, Crane-man. Their simple life is beautifully evoked. Tree-ear's ambition is to become a master potter, like the fascinating Min, but he faces many challenges on the way. There are several emotionally powerful scenes, and Korean mythology and Buddhist traditions weave in and out of the plot. The author evidently knows a great deal about pottery, and there are several passages describing the process; while some of these are extremely interesting, others may be too lengthy and detailed to entirely engage the reader. However, this is a finely crafted novel and a beautiful study in character that transports the reader into an unfamiliar world and makes that world real and vivid. It is an appealing tale of friendship, youthful naïveté, sadness, simple happiness and hope.

JMi

Bolgchaint agus Scéalta Eile

Ré Ó Laighléis
Móinín, ISBN 0-9532777-3-9, €7 (clúdach bog/pbk)

In this collection of short stories Ré Ó Laighléis, true to form, raises many controversial issues, such as Irish insular attitudes towards foreigners, as seen in the story 'Ball'. What is particularly commendable about this collection, however, is that children are empowered to recognise and combat injustice themselves. Thus, in 'Focalghníomh', children who make hurtful, racist remarks to a young refugee are encouraged to revise their attitudes due to the words and actions of younger children. Throughout this collection, Ó Laighéis is particularly sensitive to those who have been unfairly marginalised, perhaps most notably in the story 'Suáilce'.

Ar an iomlán is cnuasach an-dóchasach é seo. Tá teachtaireacht láidir sna scéalta gur féidir leis an duine aonair difríocht shuntasach a dhéanamh. Sa scéal 'Cor', mar shampla, feictear an tábhacht a bhaineann leis an ngníomh is lú agus creidtear i míorúiltí mar a léiríonn an príomh-scéal, 'Bolgchaint'.

ÁNicG

Boy Kills Man

Matt Whyman
Hodder, ISBN 0-340-88195-X, £5.99 (pbk)

Shortlisted for the 2004 Booktrust Teenage Prize, this much-praised and critically acclaimed book is worthy of every plaudit that has been heaped on it. From the very start, it is uncompromising in the reality it presents and is not an easy read. Shorty and Alberto are twelve years old, are best friends and live in the ghetto of Medellín, Colombia, where they run wild around the streets. The friendship changes when the local gangland boss recruits Alberto. When his friend goes missing, Shorty has to reassess his own world and his place in it. The lack of choices facing children and their families in the developing world is fiercely brought home to the reader: this is how life really is for many young people in another part of our increasingly small world. No quarter is given to the reader as the short and brutal life of the child assassin is chillingly, heartbreakingly and most eloquently described. We get a glimpse into the reality of the ruthless and destructive society these children inhabit – a society we can only see though a small window opened by the author within the pages of this book.

FO'S

Brilliance of the Moon

Lian Hearn
Young Picador, ISBN 0-330-41350-3, £6.99 (pbk)

To understand the people of a country, one should first understand the history of that country. Our pasts shape us as individuals; equally, the historic past shapes a nation. Its art, music, literature, rituals and beliefs all colour the particular ethnicity that makes the country, and its people, unique. In this, the third book of the Tales of the Otori, the author has provided a vivid description of an ancient Japan, with its strict code of loyalty and honour. The feudal system, the notion of outcasts and the secret influence of Christianity all make this an enthralling read. Through the story, there is also the powerful force of Takeo's love for Kaede, and the emotion of their eventual reunion, though both have been disfigured. With this love story, the amazing abilities of those born into the Tribe, the bloody battles and the devastating earthquakes, there is something for every reading taste. This story provides ample material for exploring the ideas of loyalty, honour to the point of suicide, and attitudes to those on the edges of society.

JD

Caught in the Crossfire

Alan Gibbons
Orion, ISBN 1-84255-096-9, £4.99 (pbk)

Detailing the events that lead to mayhem on the streets of a British town when racists and a Muslim community come into violent conflict, this novel wears its political heart on its sleeve. There is no doubt on which side the author stands: against racism. There is also no doubt about where he lays the main blame for racist violence. And yet, this is no one-sided polemic. The frustration, anger and self-loathing that lead to racist activity among a disenfranchised and despairing white population are clearly outlined, as are the machinations of a politically astute outsider, who manoeuvres an apathetic community into ethnic hatred. The Muslim community in the novel is saved from unrealistic saintliness by the reaction of its young men to provocation, and they are shown not to be above stupid and dangerous actions either. This novel deals with social issues head-on, but it doesn't feel like a lecture: it is absorbing, carefully plotted and written in a pacy and readable style. The whole book consists of easily digested short scenes, written in the present tense and intercut in the manner of a TV drama, which will help to hold the interest not only of committed readers, but also of young people who come to reading more reluctantly.

SP

Chandra

Frances Mary Hendry
Oxford University Press, ISBN 0-19-27347-9, £4.99 (pbk)

Chandra is eleven, and an excellent student at her Delhi high school. She's a good daughter too, though more modern than her father would like her to be, so the whole family is delighted when a marriage is arranged for her with Roop, a 'modern-minded' sixteen-year-old. Only her grandmother casts any doubt on the match, and worries about her going to live so far away. Since she won't be living with her husband until her schooling is finished, Chandra returns to school after the wedding and throws herself into her studies so that she will be able to help Roop with the chain of hotels he plans to run. But all her dreams for her future are destroyed when Roop dies very suddenly: as a widow, she is now the property of her husband's very traditional family. Trapped, miserable and far from home on their farm in Rajasthan, Chandra makes a daring escape across the desert. But even back in Delhi she's not safe – will her family take her in, or will Roop's family catch up with her? This is an exciting story, with a resourceful and appealing heroine, that takes a sympathetic look at tradition, arranged marriages and honour. There is a glossary at the back of the book, along with a brief outline of Hindi beliefs.

HC

Chinese Cinderella and the Secret Dragon Society

Adeline Yen Mah
Puffin, ISBN 0-14-1314966, £5.99 (pbk)

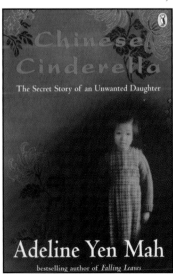

Set in Shanghai during World War II and based on true events, this story concerns young Ye Xian, a girl whose parents have rejected her and who joins a troupe of orphans and displaced children in the Academy of Martial Arts under the tutelage of Grandma Wu. The children learn kung fu, how to cook delicious Chinese meals and how to use the Yi Jing, the sacred book of Chinese wisdom (known in the West as the I Ching), and later they become involved in the rescue of American airmen involved on the Chinese side in the war against Japan. As a young readers' introduction to Chinese culture and history that goes much deeper than the average kung-fu movie, this book scores highly. It is sprinkled with short phrases of Chinese, and the reader encounters ideas central to Chinese philosophy and religion. This is all wrapped up in an adventure story that allows the main characters to star in exciting wartime exploits and help to fight their country's enemies. As a novel, it has many flaws – weak characterisation, an incredible plot, narrative awkwardness, poor pacing, large chunks of unconvincing dialogue, ill-digested research and an embarrassing level of didacticism – but young readers may forgive those faults and just enjoy the adventure.

SP

Coram Boy

Jamila Gavin
Egmont, ISBN 1-4052-1282-9, £5.99 (pbk)

At once a tale of two boys and of fathers and sons, this Whitbread Children's Book of the Year is an adventure story where love, hatred, corruption and childhood vie for survival. A Thomas Coram did found a hospital for 'deserted children' in the 1740s, and it still exists; but this is a novel portraying an underbelly of unrelenting greed, facilitated by Otis, who uses the hospital as a 'honey trap of deceit'. Otis induces poverty-stricken and tragic mothers to believe their children and babies will be safely brought to Coram – but money is his all, and many children never reach the hospital. This is both an uncomfortable read and an exciting page-turner. The characters, young and old, wonderful and utterly dreadful, are keenly portrayed and credible: Toby, from a slave ship; Aaron, heir to an estate; Alexander, who abandons his inheritance for a career in music; Mezhak, tragic son of the evil Otis; Melissa, Aaron's young mother; and several others. Gavin does not shirk from showing us that, while love can triumph, the harsh real world allows this evil child-killer and slave-trader to disappear unpunished. This is powerful historical fiction, haunting and compelling.

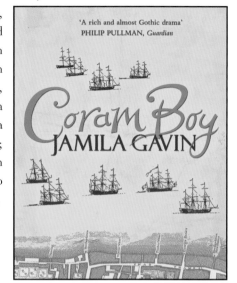

SC

Daughter of the Wind

Suzanne Fisher Staples
Walker Books, ISBN 0-7445-9011-6, £4.99 (pbk)

This wonderful and highly praised book centres around the lives of a nomadic family in the Cholistan desert of Pakistan. Shabanu is the twelve-year-old daughter, and it is through her eyes that we get a glimpse of her life, both within her family and in the desert. The narrative is a coming-of-age story where the members of Shabanu's family try to steer her away from her independence and her free thinking and prepare her for her life as a teenage bride and mother. Her free spirit is contrasted with the more docile personality of her older sister Phulan. The tension between what Shabanu wants for herself and the life her family has mapped out for her provides the centre for the story. The telling of Shabanu's story is both real and raw and challenges the reader to re-think beliefs around tradition and individual rights, especially those of women.

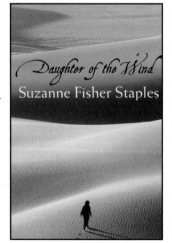

FO'S

Daughter of Venice

Donna Jo Napoli
Walker Books, ISBN 0-7445-9080-9, £5.99 (pbk)

Donata Mocenigo is the daughter of a sixteenth-century Venetian nobleman, and she wants more from life than the future that her very restrictive social and economic position seems to offer her. This book is a deeply interesting exploration of the hierarchical society and religious structures of Venice at the time of the Inquisition, but it is not the worthy treatise this makes it sound. It does struggle a little in the early chapters, where dialogue is unconvincingly used to fill in background information; but once the mise-en-scène is complete, the reader is quickly drawn to overlook this initial awkwardness as the plot gathers pace and the mystery deepens. As the novel winds to its conclusion, the heroine does not get to marry the man she loves – the outcome modern readers might expect, but one that would have been unthinkable in Donata's circumstances. She does, however, get to have a far more absorbing and satisfying future than most young women of her time and background; and yet it is entirely credible that this extraordinary young woman could have forced the hand of fate as she does. An excellent historical novel, which touches on issues such as religious and social divisions and treats them with a refreshing respect for contemporary values.

SP

Divided City

Theresa Breslin
Doubleday, ISBN 0-385-60767-9, £10.99 (hbk)

It is May, the Orange marching season is just beginning and feelings are running high between Celtic and Rangers fans in a contemporary Glasgow still split by old differences of race and religion. Two young boys, supporters of opposing teams, take the first tentative steps towards friendship after one of them witnesses a horrific attack on Kyoul, a Muslim asylum-seeker and illegal entrant to the city. Their prejudices and passions are dealt with honestly: this is a book that sets racism and sectarianism in a domestic context and shows how prejudice can go unquestioned in the most ordinary of homes. Only Graham's love for his Granda makes him think seriously about joining the Orange march – the old man would be so disappointed if Graham refused to wear the sash and take part in the walk. There is humour here too (in Scotland, Joe's grandmother has been told, there's 'a Catholic and a Protestant way to hang up your drawers'), though there is a sinister undercurrent. Ultimately, this is an optimistic story about football, friendship and hope for the future.

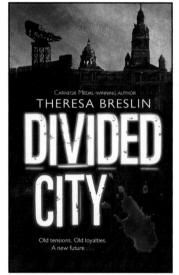

LM

Dream On

Bali Rai
Barrington Stoke, ISBN 1-84299-195-7, £4.99 (pbk)

This story centres around the friendship among three teenage boys from an Asian community as they grow up in London. Their lives and aspirations revolve around becoming professional footballers, but they have to contend with the cultural assumptions of family and with racism from rival school students. The relationship between the central character, Baljit, and his father, as they struggle with their differing assumptions and needs, is tenderly evoked. Baljit has to be resourceful with his family and exercise duplicity in order to follow his chosen independent path, but he does achieve harmony and gain acceptance in the end. Although the story does not probe issues in any great depth, the friends' determination as they successfully make their own way and integrate with mainstream society is well described. The value of the bonds of friendship across class and culture is emphasised. The realities and difficulties of immigrant communities, as they struggle to adapt to and be accepted by mainstream society, lie at the heart of this simple story.

CQ

From Out of the Shadows

Jamila Gavin
Egmont, ISBN 1-4052-0280-7, £4.99 (pbk)

This is a vivid and imaginative collection of short stories that moves between English, Indian and Celtic settings and between the present, the distant past and the future. The author successfully mixes elements of myth and folktale from different cultures to produce some vibrant new tales. The tone varies from the powerfully mythic to the light-hearted and comical. Some stories are more successful than others: the opening, science-fictional 'The Desert Singer' is urgent and compact, leaving the reader to draw his or her own conclusions; 'The Paradise Carpet', on the other hand, may seem predictable and sentimental to some readers, while the whimsical 'Mona' seems a little out of place, as the rest of the collection is anything but whimsical. Although the variety of settings and forms shows the author's great imaginative skill, this book doesn't really work that well as a cohesive collection. There is little sense of continuity from story to story, and no obvious pattern or structure in the ordering of the stories. Each narrative does provide unusual and interesting reading, however, and most readers will find something to enjoy and contemplate in this wide-ranging collection.

NM

Grass for his Pillow

Lian Hearn
Young Picador, ISBN 0-330-41526-3, £6.99 (pbk)

This is the second volume in the 'Tales of the Otori' trilogy, which is set in a fictional Japan. The huge list of characters may appear somewhat daunting at first, but persistence pays, as this is a good read. Essentially it is the story of two young lovers, Otori Takeo and Shirakawa Kaede, who have been separated by war and formal codes of

allegiance. Takeo's physical powers are reminiscent of the magical martial arts shown in the film *Crouching Tiger, Hidden Dragon*, and this, with the finely observed description of character and landscape, adds to the vivid narrative. We follow their dangerous journeys alternately until finally they meet again and marry, despite the wrath and enmity that they know will follow them – in the third part of the trilogy. The story is full of cruelty, murder, allusions to torture and rules that must be followed on pain of death, but it is at the points where individual human feelings and needs strain against society's strict feudal system and warrior code that the story really comes alive, and we really care about the protagonists.

LJ

Hite

Kate Saksena
Bloomsbury, ISBN 0-7475-6899-5, £5.99 (pbk)

Lee – victim of his father's violence, bullied into criminal complicity by the local gang, struggling at school and in trouble for absenteeism – escapes for peace and quiet to the roof of the block of flats where he lives. His sole act of self-assertion is to leave his 'tag', his own particular design in graffiti, on ever-higher buildings. The novel oscillates between the bleak misery of his father's brutal beatings and the moments of warmth and hope arising from his contact with Ruby (a girl he meets on the roof), his grandmother and his classmate Vivienne. When Lee rescues a family from a burning building and, weeks later, despite all his instincts, does the same for his father, he finds himself not hailed as a hero but under suspicion of arson. The understated, bald

Grief, gangs, graffiti. Should Lee fight it?

narrative illustrates brilliantly how random adult responses can seem from the point of view of an intellectually challenged young man.

AP

Lost for Words

Elizabeth Lutzeier
Macmillan, ISBN 0-330-39820-2, £4.99 (pbk)

Set in Bengal and London, this is the story of Aysha and her struggle to adjust to her new life in a place where she cannot speak the language. Aysha's father has been living in England, sending money back to the family, ever since she was tiny. The story opens as he arrives home for the first time in six years, laden with presents for the extended family. He appears to be very prosperous, and he has decided to bring his wife and daughter back to London with him. But London is not the paradise he has painted, and Aysha has to grow up quickly, helping her mother to negotiate the shopping streets and, worse, witnessing her parents' humiliation at the hands of housing officers and the like. She battles to cope with the insults that come even from well-meaning people, and to deal with the constant clashes that living between two cultures entails. This is a warm story that does not shy away from realistic depiction of racism as experienced by Asian families in England.

LJ

Love my Enemy

Kate MacLachlan
Andersen Press, ISBN 1-84270-340-4, £5.99 (pbk)

A sometimes bleak contemporary story of life in today's Northern Ireland, post-peace agreement. The guns have fallen silent, but old hatreds resist resolution, particularly for the young adults reared in an atmosphere of deadly violence. MacLachlan has woven together the disparate lives of teenager Zee and her deeply traumatised brother Gary, who saw their RUC policeman father shot dead in front of them, with that of Tasha, newly arrived from England with her mother, who works resettling refugees, and her new stepfather Miguel, a Bosnian refugee. Conor is the Catholic neighbour who falls in love with Zee, while Tasha sets her sights on the psychotic Gary. Inevitably, trouble and tragedy ensue as both sides struggle to understand the new realities. Shortlisted for the Children's Books Ireland/Bisto awards, this is a white-knuckle journey, ending in rescue and redemption, which will challenge readers and perhaps leave them understanding a little more about the futility of sectarianism.

CC

Mo Chroí san Afraic

Victor Mora, arna aistriú ag Carl Mac Gabhann
agus Tomás Mac Síomóin
An Gúm, ISBN 1-85791-470-8, €5.95 (clúdach bog/pbk)

Mo Chroí san Afraic, a translation from Catalan, is a hard-hitting novel set in Zaire. Power and greed are the driving impulses of Mora's novel, which deals primarily with the rampant exploitation of Zaire's natural resources and speaks out very forcibly about the far-reaching consequences of the corruption endemic in Central Africa. The title relates to Tónaí, a young Catalan who must save his friends from certain death at the hands of the formidable Madame Singh, who is involved in the illegal abduction of wild animals from the jungle.

Is trí shúile an fhir óig, Tónaí, a fheicimid tírdhreach agus áilleacht na hAfraice. Is trína shúile siúd chomh maith a thagaimid chun tuisceana ar chastacht na polaitíochta. Baineann an t-úrscéal le forbairt Tónaí: ag deireadh an úrscéil bíonn tuiscint níos iomláine aige ar an saol, agus a chéad bhlaiseadh de chúrsaí grá faighte aige. Úrscéal fiúntach é seo, atá feiliúnach do dhéagóirí óga, agus teachtaireacht láidir ann.

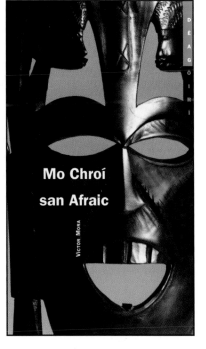

ÁNicG

Maistín

Peter Jan Rens, arna aistriú ag Alex Hijmans
Cló Iar-Chonnachta, ISBN 1-902420-44-6, €8 (clúdach bog/pbk)

This is the story of Willem-Jan, who, in common with other boys of ten and a half, is developing his own identity and learning independence. To this end, he changes his name from Willem-Jan to Maistín (Bully), creating discord between himself and his parents. He runs away to the big city and develops a strong friendship with Ine, a girl six years older than he. He also befriends a drunken down-and-out, Groothoff. Fortunately, after much mishap and adventure, Maistín is reunited with his parents, Ine receives the help she needs and all ends well.

Scéal é seo faoi bhuachaill óg, Willem-Jan, atá ag iarraidh a fhéiniúlacht agus a phearsantacht féin a fhorbairt. Nuair a athraíonn sé a ainm go Maistín, éiríonn idir é agus a thuismitheoirí. Éalaíonn sé ón teach agus téann sé go dtí an chathair mhór. Éiríonn sé an-chairdiúil le striapach óg, Íne. Cabhraíonn fear siúil, meisceoir darbh ainm Groothoff, leis chomh maith. Tá mar a bheadh athrach clainne anois ag Maistín. Tar éis dóibh a lán de shuaitheadh an tsaoil a chur díobh, déanann Maistín athmhuintearas lena thuismitheoirí, faigheann Íne an chabhair is gá agus tá gach rud ina cheart arís.

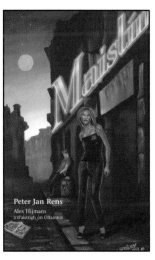

CQ

Motherland

Vineeta Vijayaraghavan
The Chicken House, ISBN 1-904442-15-3, £5.99 (pbk)

Through the skilful piling of detail upon telling detail, this assured and wonderfully insightful novel recreates a sensuous India and a restrictive Indian society to which the protagonist, Maya, returns from her home in the United States to spend what is to be her last summer of childhood. The subtle interweaving of politically motivated violence, suggestive of revolutionary change, prepares the reader for the painful process of Maya's maturation and her personal fight for freedom. Here, in the place where she grew up, the long-established values instilled in her intermingle and occasionally clash with the liberality offered her in the West. The eventual relinquishing of old certainties, symbolised by the death of her beloved grandmother, ensures Maya is free to construct an adult identity that comprises influences from both her homeland and her adopted country.

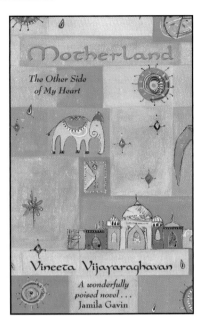

CR

Mud City

Deborah Ellis
Oxford University Press, ISBN 0-19-275 376-2, £4.99 (pbk)

Exiled from her home in Afghanistan to a widows' compound in Pakistan, Shauzia finds life anything but easy. Having been denied payment for work, she decides to leave the encampment for France, bringing only her loyal dog Jasper for company. To finance her trip, she first visits Peshawar, where she solicits work from local shopkeepers while spending her nights sleeping rough on the streets. After a run-in with police, she is imprisoned briefly before being rescued by an American engineer and his wife, who agree to take her in. Ellis rightly chooses against an easy solution to Shauzia's plight, and when she invites the local homeless community to dine and wash themselves in her proxy family's home, the altruism of her adoptive parents quickly becomes strained. Soon Shauzia finds herself homeless again and returning to the compound from which she fled. *Mud City* is an unsentimental and objective account that stresses the indomitable spirit of its heroine over the cruelty of war. As such, it is a welcome eye-opener for young readers who may be understandably complacent about their comfortable lives in the West.

Out of the Flames

Vincent McDonnell
The O'Brien Press, ISBN 0-86278-764-5, €6.95 (pbk)

In a dramatic opening, the reader is plunged straight into an African garden where Maria witnesses the brutal slaying of her mother. This is also where the reader first encounters the frightening character of Kegale, a key figure in the Malangan secret police. Fearing for Maria's safety, her father arranges for her to seek refuge in Ireland. She ends up in the little community of Culduagh, where McDonnell sensitively deals with prejudices and tension between the locals and the asylum-seekers and refugees. The plot is further developed by the clever use of a local 'piseog' concerning Dubhana, 'the dark skinned woman with red hair, who has come to seek vengeance for the disturbance of her resting place'. A local boy, David, who also has many family issues to sort out, befriends Maria. Tension increases as David rescues Maria from local youths, false accusations are made against the refugees and, finally, Kegale arrives in Ireland. This is a book that will be enjoyed by those who like a fast-paced read about differences, heroes and thugs. Older readers may find the final chapter, which overplays sentimentality, unnecessary. A pity really, as it does detract from an otherwise good read.

BC

Peace Weavers

Julia Jarman
Andersen Press, ISBN 1-84270-295-5, £5.99 (hbk)

When Hilde's mother departs for Baghdad to protest against the Iraqi war, she leaves her son and disgruntled adolescent daughter with their estranged father on an American military base in England. Here – exposed to the views of those who share neither her nationality nor her anti-war sentiments, and to the attentions of Friedman, whose fighter-pilot father is killed in the conflict – Hilde begins to change her perspective, embracing human complexities and abandoning simplistic notions of morality. This story of burgeoning love and of Hilde's desire for an end to personal and global conflict is set against the discovery of the sixth-century skeleton of a 'peace weaver' whose concerns, we discover, parallel those of Hilde; the peace weaver haunts the teenager and is instrumental in her transformation. The strength of this novel lies in the author's ability to successfully suggest the multifarious nature of youthful idealism and the magnetic quality of first sexual attraction.

CR

Pictures from the Fire

Gaye Hicyilmaz
Orion, ISBN 1-85881-896-6, £4.99 (pbk)

The novel opens with the words, 'She was locked in again.' For almost the entire story, Emilia is alone in a yellow-painted room in a German asylum hostel. She is ignored by her parents, and only with her younger brother does she have a form of covert communication. Emilia Radu is an outsider within her own family. Through her secretly drawn picture diary, Emilia reveals her past as a gypsy child in Bucharest, the journey to England and the events that force her family to move on again. Emilia's self-esteem is very low; but, like her father, she does have a vision of a better life and is prepared to take her chance of freedom. Through Emilia's story, the reader is given a glimpse of the circumstances that cause families to leave their homelands and the hostility they may face in another country.

RH

Skin Deep

edited by Tony Bradman
Puffin, ISBN 0-141-31505-9, £4.99 (pbk)

These collected stories, with their vastly different settings, share the theme of racism and the cruel and senseless divisions it creates. A maid in nineteenth-century Sydney suffers double discrimination for being an Aborigine and a woman, as well as the stigma of being a prisoner's wife. A boy sorts through rubbish in a dump in Brazil in order to

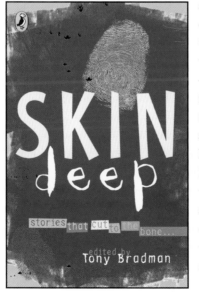

scrape a living. Two sisters whose different skin colours drive them apart, a family torn between China and Japan, an Israeli and a Palestinian boy who have more in common than they'll ever know – all suffer their own personal pain because of the intolerance of others and their own prejudices. Some stories are much stronger than others – a few are very obviously written for the sole purpose of highlighting a theme and have little literary merit. But the collection would be invaluable to teachers wishing to start a class discussion, and overall it achieves its goal: it raises awareness of the racism experienced by different groups, throughout the world and throughout human history, through the stories of the young.

NMac a'B

Surprising Joy

Valerie Bloom
Macmillan, ISBN 0-330-39860-1, £4.99 (pbk)

This account of a young girl coming to terms with a series of new identities is written in an engaging, defamiliarising, first-person Jamaican *patois*. Brought up by her grandmother in Jamaica, Joy dreams of following her emigrant mother to London. On arrival there, she finds herself expected to accept a stranger as her mother; the person she believed to be her mother is revealed to be her aunt. Conflicts of emotion, language and identity are handled in carefully, sometimes comically evoked accounts of idiolect and intimate exchange. Compromises at home and among extended family are juxtaposed with those demanded at school. Bloom's facility as a poet informs the economy of style and emotional range here, and Joy's first-person narrative leaves the reader with little choice but to face intrinsic issues of similarity and difference as directly as the character herself.

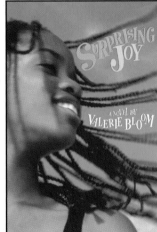

AP

The Defender

Alan Gibbons
Orion, ISBN 1-84255-098-5, £4.99 (pbk)

At one level this is a tightly written, exciting thriller in which Ian Kincaid finds his teen routine – trying to grow up, learn at school and impress girls – brutally disrupted by forces from his father's past. It is a good thriller, but it is much more than that. For one thing, the father-son role is reversed, in both moral and practical terms. The boy is literally father to the man. It is also a story that grows out of the Northern Ireland troubles. Ian's dad, Kenny, has a secret loyalist paramilitary past, has betrayed his former comrades, and lives a haunted and hunted life in England. Stereotyping of all kinds is carefully avoided here, and the humanity of both former terrorist and RUC officer is admitted equally. Above all, the teenage hero is allowed to grow in unpromising circumstances.

CK

The Gods and their Machines

Oisín McGann
The O'Brien Press, ISBN 0-86278-833-1, €6.95 (pbk)

In a vigorous and intelligent fantasy with modern political and religious connections, three young people face the ultimate physical and spiritual challenges. Chamus is a trainee fighter pilot from Altima; Riadni is a rebellious and driven young girl from repressive Bartokhrin; and Benyan is training in a rebel camp on her family's land. But soon she and Chamus are on the run for their lives. The novel's narrative lines are direct, and the action is well shaped for page-turning discovery. In our 'war on terror' era, McGann has not shirked the demons of fanaticism, murder and betrayal, nor the entanglements of personal and family relationships. The story holds its sense of human dignity in the face of relentless brutality and natural evil. Both Riadni and Chamus find time, on the run from their killer hunters, to discover the fragility of truth, the brutality of history and the bonds of cultures. There are moments of writing brilliance. The Blessing of the Martyrs ritual and Benyan's final suicide mission are powerfully crafted; the parallel spirit and physical worlds are superbly integrated, persuasive, even seductive. An accomplished work of fiction, by a writer in control of both his materials and his readers.

SC

ILLUSTRATIONS FROM THE GODS AND THEIR MACHINES

The Heaven Shop

Deborah Ellis
Oxford University Press, ISBN 0-19-275435-1, £4.99 (pbk)

Despite the loss of their mother, Binti, her brother Kwasi and their sister have a bright future ahead of them – until their father dies from AIDS. Now orphaned and separated amongst uncaring relatives, stripped of all the human complexity of needs and desires by the label of AIDS, they struggle to retain a sense of who they once were. Binti, the central character, is proud, arrogant and very selfish but still remains attractive and interesting. With her, we learn the value of solidarity and the preciousness of every life. The story of Binti and her struggle to rediscover her own sense of self-worth is told against the backdrop of Malawi's struggle to survive the loss of doctors, nurses, teachers and civil servants through the ravages of AIDS, as care workers die faster than they can be replaced. It is a story of the courage and endurance of the children and of the older generation that is left to take on the burden of care. The central theme is fear of AIDS, rather than AIDS itself, and the corrosive effect that this fear has on the bonds of family and society. It is told in a sparse and economical narrative that succeeds in personalising the issue of global responsibility of care for the orphans of AIDS in Africa.

MM

The Kin

Peter Dickinson
Macmillan, ISBN 0-330-39225-5, £6.99 (pbk)

The Kin describes a group of people in 'Africa, about two hundred thousand years ago'. They have language, mythology, and ritual. The novel focuses on five children: Suth, Noli, Tinu, Mana and Otan, all from the Moonhawk clan. As they leave their ancestral lands searching for new 'Good Places', they encounter different groups of people at various stages of development, with various beliefs and customs. Dickinson imagines these early cultures and communities very successfully, paying great attention to origin myths, social codes and rituals. The book's language is constructed to reflect the knowledge and ideas such cultures might have had. This language is not always successful, however. The narrating voice uses more complex language than the protagonists, who are given very limited patterns of speech and seem flat and only crudely individuated as a result. Coming of age, sexual experience, even childbirth and parenthood move the plot along without much exploration at the level of individual emotion. However, this is a highly absorbing novel. The world it presents is constructed with care, ambition and imagination. It should appeal to those teenagers who are already enthusiastic readers, and especially to those who enjoy reading science fiction or fantasy stories.

NM

The Love Bean

Siobhán Parkinson
The O'Brien Press, ISBN 0-86278-772-6, €6.95 (pbk)

Parkinson is an accomplished writer whose apprehension of what a story can do is sophisticated, and who pushes the boundaries beyond the familiar. Confronted with an Ireland in the throes of change, she weaves two stories about twins faced with the arrival of foreign 'smashers', separated by two thousand years. Add epilogues from *Romeo and Juliet*, and you have a cautionary tale about ancient grudge and new mutiny. Twin stories about twins provide the writer with a clever plot device. Twins are similar in appearance yet engage differently with the world, underlining the superficiality of appearances. The conceit implies that we who have ancient Irish lineage and presume a shared national identity are more various than impressions suggest. By contrast, the obvious cultural distinctiveness of Tito, the recently arrived refugee in the story, need be no barrier to a new Irish future. Paralleling Julia and Lydia's modern story is that of Sun'va and Eva, twins who encounter Flavius, a young Roman, member of a fictitious party invading ancient Ireland. The two stories are unlikely mirror images of each other, with historical context creating critical distance. Parkinson is successful in this important respect: she is sufficiently accurate and specific about contexts to persuade the reader of the tale's verisimilitude. Ireland's history may have much to tell about current intercultural dramas.

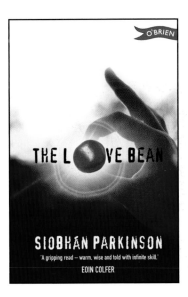

MST

The Wheel of Surya

Jamila Gavin
Egmont, ISBN 0-7497-4744-7, £4.99 (pbk)

Marvinder and Jaspal live in the Punjab with their mother Jhoti. Their father Govind has gone to England to study, encouraged by a British teacher living in India with his wife and children. However, India gains independence from Britain and civil war breaks out. As they escape, the children become separated from their mother and must 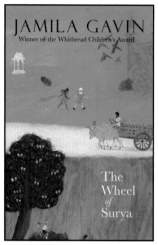 make a traumatic and remarkable journey across India and on to Britain in search of their father. While the opening chapters provide thought-provoking details on the Indian social system and its consequences for Jhoti and her family, their life in Britain has its own share of trauma, exploitation and discoveries.

JD

Walking a Tightrope: New Writing from Asian Britain

edited by Rehana Ahmed
Young Picador, ISBN 0-330-41566-2, £9.99 (pbk)

Four of these ten stories by Asian writers resident in England explore, through first-person narrators, the tensions between loyalty to family and the choices to be made among the available British micro-cultures. Of the remaining six, one recounts a bitter tale of domestic violence, another the loss of a brother, a hero-worshipped RAF pilot; both are permeated with a dreadful sense of alienation. Two more stories use fantasy to address, not without humour, the impossibility of communication between cultures. A ninth, 'Yellow Dog', beautifully describes the competition between practicality and pity among the very poorest in a small Indian town, and the unfreezing of the most obdurate of hearts. The tenth, 'Tsuru', uses myth to inform and untangle complications of love, lust, jealousy and friendship across cultures. The collection as a whole draws attention to the enormous diversity of form, character and situation within Asian writing abroad.

AP

Tribal Scars

Patrick Devaney
Mentor Books, ISBN 1-84210-250-8, €6.95 (pbk)

The main action of *Tribal Scars* revolves around Aidan, a fourteen-year-old African-Irish boy, and his estranged grandfather, Senator Tadhg Higgins, who refuses to acknowledge him. Aidan lives in relative poverty with his Irish mother, while Senator Higgins is a wealthy landowner bent on developing his estate into a world-class golf course, an ambition that draws him into violent conflict with eco-warriors. The book presents a depressing picture of life in a typical Irish town – drugs are readily available, gangs of thugs make life miserable for teachers and other pupils, and casual racism abounds – but there's also friendship, loyalty and idealism. Aidan's ethnicity brings a fresh perspective to the story; he identifies more with his Irish classmates than with the African asylum-seekers in his school, but racist factions within the school see them as 'all the same'. However, a major weakness in the book is that both Aidan's father and the asylum-seekers come from an imaginary African country, 'Nirambia': the opportunity for the reader to learn about other cultures would have been much enhanced either by the use of a real country or by an explanatory note separating fact from fiction and explaining a little about the cultures drawn on for the book. Overall, though, *Tribal Scars* is a gritty, realistic novel that will particularly appeal to teenage boys.

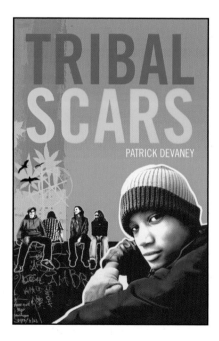

HC

Web of Lies

Beverley Naidoo
Puffin Books, ISBN 0-141-31466-4, £4.99 (pbk)

This is a sequel to the author's Carnegie Medal winner, *The Other Side of Truth*, which depicts a journalist and his two young adolescent children, Sade and Femi, fleeing to England after the assassination of his wife in his native Nigeria. *Web of Lies* revolves around Femi's experiences of being exploited and corrupted by a local gang in his adopted country. He narrowly escapes being stabbed and is suspected by the police of having perpetrated a near-fatal assault. Consistent with Naidoo's interweaving of English and African experiences, the brutalisation of Femi is allied to the sub-plot, which highlights the plight of Nigerian boy-soldiers. 'People in Britain need to know what's going on.' This drive to inform, which characterises Femi's father, is seemingly shared by the author and is achieved at the expense of strong characterisations and literary excellence.

CR

Yankee Girl

Mary Ann Rodman
Usborne, ISBN 0-7460-6749-6, £4.99 (pbk)

Set in 1966, *Yankee Girl* evokes, in a truthful and sensitive first-person narration, the tensions experienced by an eleven-year-old girl whose family moves to the Deep South when her father, an FBI agent, is despatched there to oversee the racial integration of local schools. Exploring questions of race alongside those of class, age and gender, Rodman's text is written out of her own experience. Dialogue and character are vivid and convincing, and the text confronts its readers with the crucial decisions to be made when a young person is torn between choosing to assimilate invisibly into a new community or consciously alienating herself by holding true to her own political and social convictions. Each chapter is headed with contemporary newspaper headlines; the text simultaneously teaches a lesson in history and pulls into sharp focus the personal decisions made daily by any young person in a politically charged situation.

AP

Wings Over Delft

Aubrey Flegg
The O'Brien Press, ISBN 0-86278-886-2, €7.95 (pbk)

In seventeenth-century Holland, in a society marked by religious and class divisions, a young woman is coming of age. Louise Eeden is the daughter of a local master potter and is widely believed to be engaged to Reynier DeVries, a childhood friend whose father owns a prosperous delftware factory. Her father, an amateur scientist and a free thinker, travels widely and introduces Louise to new developments and concepts. As she reluctantly agrees to sit for a portrait with painter Master Haitink, she embarks on her own voyage, one of personal discovery, accompanied by Haitink's apprentice, Pieter. Through the eyes of Pieter and Louise, the reader questions social and class divisions and considers matters of science and art, human motivation, sincerity and manipulation, truth and deceit. As she attends a Mass in a secret church, Louise, who has been raised as a Protestant, finds herself on the 'brink of a great discovery' and, with her, the reader is brought to an increased understanding of difference, prejudice and tolerance. The questioning and open minds of both Louise and Pieter have much to teach the reader about tolerance and acceptance, and ultimately about love, death and life. A deserving winner of the Bisto Book of the Year Award 2004.

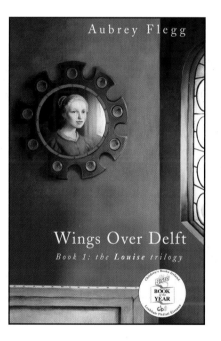

LM

PETER HEANEY

Standing in African Shoes

Enabling students to understand the perspective of others is one of the key factors in intercultural and development education. This project allowed students in Northern Ireland and South Africa to discuss their responses to **The Cinnamon Tree** *via the internet.*

IT WAS ALICE who asked, 'What is the use of a book without pictures or conversations?' identifying the essence of a book as communication – with the characters, with the author and ultimately with oneself.[1]

This is a brief impression of a project that brought together schools under the management of the Western Education and Library Board, in Northern Ireland, and schools in South Africa, through the Think.com website. Through this project, students who were reading Aubrey Flegg's book *The Cinnamon Tree* (2000) were able to communicate over a ten-to-twelve week period. *The Cinnamon Tree* charts the story of a young African girl, Yola, and her journey to recovery following mutilation in a landmine accident. The book is suitable for upper primary or lower second-level children.

With the increased availability of internet communications technology (ICT) in schools, there is now the opportunity to incorporate some of the possibilities this offers into the school curriculum. For this project, Think.com served as the communication platform. Think.com is a virtual learning environment (VLE) that is supported by the Oracle Corporation and is freely available to schools. C2k (Classroom 2000) also supported the work. C2k is a Northern Ireland curriculum support agency, which promotes the use of ICT in schools.

The principal aim of the project was to create a dialogue, based on the book, between the students from the different schools. Through the website the children could discuss *The Cinnamon Tree* with one another, the author and the characters; the author, Aubrey Flegg, also took on the persona of Yola. Each student could set up a personal area on the Think.com website in which they could publish their thoughts and comments, allowing the students to interact on an individual level. Navigation to one another's areas was easy. It was hoped that these interactions would lead the students to both an appreciation of one another's perspective and an awareness of their own perspective.

While the technology facilitated interaction to a level and degree that would have otherwise been impossible to achieve, the class teachers helped the students to develop the skills required for meaningful communication. Considerations for the students were:

> What do I want to say?
> Is what is being heard what I am trying to say?
> How will a reply form from what I am saying?

These questions helped to develop the students' awareness of the ways in which they communicate with others.

As the project progressed, students showed an increased willingness to engage in a debate and express an opinion. These opinions showed evidence of research and the benefit of a considered position. In the tone and focus of the children's questions and exchanges their empathy with both Yola and one another

In the tone and focus of the children's questions and exchanges, their empathy with both Yola and one another became very apparent

became very apparent. Some of the questions became quite poignant: 'Yola, what is it like to lose your leg?' 'Yola, did you lose your leg in real life?' Skilled responses from the author opened many opportunities in class to discuss and consider life with a range of disabilities and difference.

The benefit of the structure – both the Internet and the classroom management aspects – was that it facilitated an exchange. The focus and thrust of the exchange was determined by curriculum considerations.

The opportunity to construct an environment where the children could interact with, challenge or support different perspectives will inevitably bring benefit to the classroom and to the children's learning. Through their discussion of *The Cinnamon Tree*, the students were encouraged to consider how they form opinions and how their opinions match the reality. They could experiment with different perspectives and in the process distil the essence of their own perspective. They were truly able to stand in African shoes to look at Yola's story.

[1] Carroll, Lewis, *Alice in Wonderland*. 1865.

BOOKS DISCUSSED IN THIS ARTICLE:
Flegg, Aubrey, *The Cinnamon Tree*. The O'Brien Press, 2000, 0862786576

SOCORRO CANO, TRANSLATED BY MOLLY O'DUFFY

Learning and Leisure: Irish Development Aid Leads the Way in Nicaragua

The library in the Environmental School, Nicaragua is an innovative development project that has the potential to effect big changes on the traditional learning and leisure habits of the students, staff and wider community. Socorro Cano discusses the opportunities the library provides for the deprived barrio in which it is situated.

SCARCE RESOURCES make schools in Nicaragua fairly forbidding places. Many classrooms contain little more than a blackboard; the children sit on the floor, and books are reserved for the teacher. If there are any supplementary books in the school, they are kept under lock and key, for fear that if the children had access to them they would be destroyed.

The Nicaraguan Environmental School (EAN), in the poor barrio of Jonathan Gonzalez in central Managua, is a welcome exception. Here, Development Cooperation Ireland has helped to fund a small library that is open to pupils, teachers, young people attending other schools and members of the community.

The aims of the library – which many might consider a luxury, in a barrio where basic needs are by no means met – are as follows:

- To support learning in the school and promote the scientific, cultural, intellectual, creative and social development of the students
- To allow students to carry out investigative and project work, especially in the school's area of expertise – environmental education
- To provide a space where books can be read aloud to children
- To help improve reading levels
- To provide enjoyment through reading
- To foster the habit of reading in the school and the community
- To provide a quiet space where children and teachers can do school-work or 'lose themselves' in books
- To act as a discovery centre and a resource for independent learning

The library contains a wide variety of books. The books most in demand are those related to language (including dictionaries), applied sciences, history, geography, civics and social studies, as well as atlases and encyclopaedias.

The innovative nature of the EAN library in the context of Nicaraguan public education cannot be overstated. Literacy levels in the country are extremely low, and adults who are literate read very little more than the Bible and newspaper headlines. Bedtime stories are practically unheard of, and most children have no access to books in the normal course of their lives. In all but the remotest parts of the country, loud music blares out from every corner, rendering reading and concentration extremely difficult. Many aspects of the EAN library – for example, encouraging reading for enjoyment, providing a quiet space for reading and study, and urging students to discover information by themselves rather than relying on teachers – are extraordinarily innovative.

The innovative nature of the EAN library in the context of Nicaraguan public education cannot be overstated

The library is also used for meetings, for cultural events and as a space in which to exhibit the children's artwork. One of the teachers doubles as the librarian, and she, along with a group of student volunteers, ensures that the rotas and rules of the library are strictly adhered to.

The library is helping to give EAN students a sense of the possibilities that books can open up to them. While this is something that many take for granted in the more privileged areas of the world, it is a gift that is, unfortunately, given to few Nicaraguan children.

Chanda's Secrets

Allan Stratton
The Chicken House, ISBN 1-904442-59-5, £5.99 (pbk)

Chanda's Secrets unashamedly sets out to make us care about the devastating effect AIDS is having in sub-Saharan Africa. Through the young narrator's eyes, we see a whole generation being lost through poverty, ignorance and fear of evil spirits. The whispers of neighbours 'spread like germs, infecting minds', yet people and priests talk  of cancer and TB, rather than of HIV. Sunday mornings are spent visiting the 'ring of death', as Chanda's friend Esther describes the circle of cemeteries surrounding the town: Esther's parents and Chanda's father, infant sister and brothers are buried in one rocky field, and every day fresh graves are added and marked with bricks on which there is no room even for names. But this is also a story about adolescence: Chanda must take responsibility for the family when she herself still needs mothering. She hears her stepfather's death described as an 'accident' and bravely declares that he died of AIDS, but finds it hard to accept the likelihood that her mother too may be dying – a secret she has been keeping even from herself. This is the story of millions of ruined lives and stolen futures that we must care about – but it is also about courage in the face of impossible odds.

LM

Checkmate

Malorie Blackman
Doubleday, ISBN 0-385-60773-3, £12.99 (hbk)

Checkmate, though it stands alone as a novel, can only really be appreciated in the context of the other books in Blackman's trilogy reviewed in this section. *Checkmate* picks up the story of Callie Rose, the mixed-race baby born of a forbidden love affair between Cross girl Sephy and Nought Callum. Callie Rose is now sixteen, an angry young woman who is the object of prejudice from both Noughts and Crosses. Though Sephy assures her daughter she is no 'halfer', but lucky enough to be able to take the best from both races and put them together to create the person she wants to be, Callie Rose herself feels that her father's legacy has left her 'with no path to follow but his', and she wants others to hurt as she does – 'a way down inside, deep rooted kind of hurt.' The book is told variously in the voices of Sephy, her mother Jasmine, her mother-in-law Meggie and a growing Callie Rose (her first contribution dates from when she is only seven); we also hear Callum's voice through letters, and Jude, Callie Rose's uncle and leader of a terrorist organisation, speaks directly to the reader. This is a thought-provoking, dramatic and moving conclusion to this best-selling trilogy.

LM

Coinnigh do Mhisneach

Sioned Wynn Jones, arna aistriú ag Diarmuid Johnson
Cló Iar-Chonnachta, ISBN 1-902420-71-3, €8 (clúdach bog/pbk)

This book, set in modern Ireland, tells the story of fifteen-year-old Máire's sexual awakening against the background of an impoverished and broken home. Máire also strikes up a friendship with Aoife, whose family is wealthy; this juxtaposition of poverty and plenty shows us the two faces of modern Ireland and the social changes afoot, with family breakdown common to rich and poor. An attractive, well-told story that concludes on a note of hope, it shows the resourcefulness of the young in the struggle for true love.

Scéal nua-aimseartha é seo, faoi Mháire, cailín sé bliana déag d'aois. Cuntas atá ann ar mhianta an ghrá agus í ag teacht in inmhe agus ar na deacrachtaí teaghlaigh atá ag Máire. Tugtar léargas dúinn ar an chultúr rachmasach Tíogar-Cheilteach atá anois sa tír agus ar an athrú sóisialta atá tagtha dá bharr. Tugtar léargas dúinn ar shaol na mbocht agus ar an saol rachmasach araon, tríd an gcairdeas idir Máire agus Aoife, cailín a bhfuil a tuismitheoirí scartha. Tá cuardach an ghrá mar phríomh-théama san úrscéal taitneamhach seo agus is deas é go gcríochnaíonn an scéal ar nóta dóchais.

CQ

Fífeanna agus Feadóga

Tomás Ó Canainn
Cló Iar-Chonnachta, ISBN 1-902420-47-0, €12 (clúdach bog/pbk)

This novel gives an effective account of the complexity and depth of the Troubles in the North. It is a story based on two teenagers in love: Sara, who is Catholic, and Roy, who is Protestant. The sharp historical inter-community conflict is shown through the eyes of the two lovers. We see the terrorism, the violence and the killing that takes place, and the author seems only too aware that history all too often repeats itself. The story finishes on a climax of tension, but there is a hint of hope: Sara is expecting a child who will have links with both traditions. This novel won the Listowel Writers' Week Prize.

Tugann an t-úrscéal éifeachtach seo léargas dúinn ar chastacht agus ar dhoimhneacht na dTrioblóidí sa Tuaisceart. Tá an scéal bunaithe ar bheirt déagóirí atá i ngrá le chéile, Sorcha ar Caitliceach í agus Roy ar Protastúnach é. Taispeántar an choimhlint ghéar stairiúil idir an dá phobal trí shúile na beirte. Feictear an sceimhlitheoireacht, an foréigean agus an marú a tharlaíonn. Druideann an scéal chun deiridh ar bharrchéim teannais. Is comhartha dóchais é go bhfuil Sorcha ag iompar clainne agus go mbainfidh an páiste leis an dá thraidisiún.

CQ

Gangsta Rap

Benjamin Zephaniah
Bloomsbury, ISBN 0-7475-6565-1, £5.99 (pbk)

Fifteen-year-old Ray is in trouble at home and at school; he's disruptive and not especially interested in learning, and his parents worry that he's a bad influence on his younger sister. The only thing he cares about is music – rap and hip-hop. When he is excluded from school, his downward spiral seems irreversible – now he's free to 'roam the streets' all day with his friends Tyrone and Prem. But help comes from an unlikely source: their 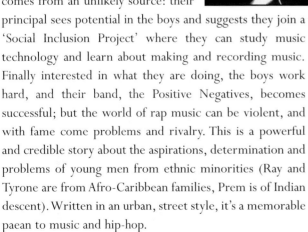 principal sees potential in the boys and suggests they join a 'Social Inclusion Project' where they can study music technology and learn about making and recording music. Finally interested in what they are doing, the boys work hard, and their band, the Positive Negatives, becomes successful; but the world of rap music can be violent, and with fame come problems and rivalry. This is a powerful and credible story about the aspirations, determination and problems of young men from ethnic minorities (Ray and Tyrone are from Afro-Caribbean families, Prem is of Indian descent). Written in an urban, street style, it's a memorable paean to music and hip-hop.

HC

Goimh agus Scéalta Eile

Ré Ó Laighléis
Móinín, ISBN 0-9532777-4-7, €7 (clúdach bog/pbk)

Shortlisted for the Children's Books Ireland/Bisto awards, these eight intriguing short stories portray modern young Irish people and their interaction with peoples of diverse backgrounds and traditions. Sometimes these young Irish find their lives enriched by co-workers and others they meet in foreign countries such as Panama; in 'Feall' the voice we hear is that of Illi Hagi, whose work colleagues can't always protect him from the taunts and jeers of his boss. The author does not shy away from depicting scenes of particularly racist  behaviour, and, in so doing, he urges readers to examine their own learned behaviour, motives and interactions with people from different backgrounds.

Ar dhéagóirí go háirithe atá *Goimh agus Scéalta Eile* dírithe. Is leabhar suimiúil é sa mhéid is go dtugann sé léargas ar shaol comhaimseartha na hÉireann, agus go príomh ar ghnéithe den saol sin atá ag déanamh tinnis don aos óg. Ocht ngearrscéal ar fad atá sa chnuasach seo, a théann i ngleic le ceist an chiníochais i measc daoine óga. Déanann an t-údar iarracht tuiscint a fháil ar údar an chiníochais sin, agus leigheas a fháil ar an scéal.

Knife Edge

Malorie Blackman
Corgi, ISBN 0-552-54892-8, £5.99 (pbk)

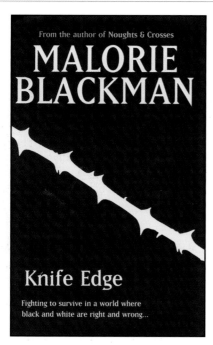

This is the second book in Blackman's 'Noughts and Crosses' trilogy (see *Noughts and Crosses* and *Checkmate*, also reviewed in this section). Though darker than the first, it is equally inspirational and flawless in its portrayal of an unjust society. Sephy now lives alone with her mixed-race baby, pursued by Callum's brother Jude, who blames her for everything that has happened to his Nought family. He is determined to destroy both Sephy and her baby, and in the process he descends into his own hell. In this distorted world, where truth and justice are defined by the Crosses, the Noughts grow daily more desperate. Alienated from both her own and Callum's family, Sephy is eaten up with guilt, a desire to atone and an overwhelming need for some form of redemption. Many key issues about the lives we all have to lead are raised in this intelligent, intensely emotional novel, which will leave the reader longing for a world that is not divided by colour or class.

CC

Noughts & Crosses

Malorie Blackman
Corgi, ISBN 0-552-54632-1, £5.99 (pbk)

Malorie Blackman has turned our known world on its head in this gripping novel, the first in a trilogy. Beware: once you start reading, you won't put it down. Sephy and Callum are inseparable as growing children, despite the fact that Sephy is a Cross from a rich, powerful and influential family, while Callum's family are white 'Noughts' struggling to survive. In this unequal world, Noughts and Crosses do not mix – but Sephy and Callum's friendship inevitably grows into forbidden love. This is a heady mix of racism, love, politics and violence, as the Noughts reach breaking point and begin to organise. The pervasive hostility of the Crosses turns to suppression, and Callum, who has the coolest head around, finds himself caught up in terrifying events brought about by Sephy's recklessness. Their love survives, but at a high price. This is as good as it gets; everyone should read it.

CC

Rani & Sukh

Bali Rai
Corgi, ISBN 0-552-54890-1, £5.99 (pbk)

This is a powerful novel about the different lives of two Punjabi families living in Britain. Fifteen-year-old Rani, beautiful and full of life, is in love with Sukh. Both are unaware of the feud 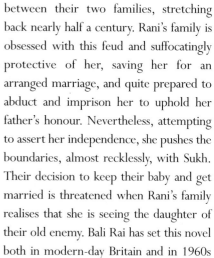 between their two families, stretching back nearly half a century. Rani's family is obsessed with this feud and suffocatingly protective of her, saving her for an arranged marriage, and quite prepared to abduct and imprison her to uphold her father's honour. Nevertheless, attempting to assert her independence, she pushes the boundaries, almost recklessly, with Sukh. Their decision to keep their baby and get married is threatened when Rani's family realises that she is seeing the daughter of their old enemy. Bali Rai has set this novel both in modern-day Britain and in 1960s Punjab, when a similar story was played out between the two families. That affair ended in a double tragedy – but both Rani and Sukh, with the support of Sukh's family, are determined to stop it happening to them. A strong story, beautifully realised.

CC

Sách Sean agus Scéalta Eile

gearrscéalta arna roghnú ag Christine Evans,
arna n-aistriú ag Micheál Ó Conghaile
Cló Iar-Chonnachta, ISBN 1-902420-58-6, €8 (clúdach bog/pbk)

This collection of short stories provides a variety of themes for teenagers facing the problems of adult life. Among the topics covered are the first job, bullying, the relationship between a mother and daughter, abortion and sexuality, and the cultivation of the inner life and identity. The stories seek to reveal the human truth at the heart of experience. Understanding does not come quickly: it is part of a process, and suffering is accordingly unavoidable, but learning is possible if we are open to it. This book was IBBY Ireland's nomination for translation in the Honour List 2002–04.

Meascán de scéalta atá anseo do dhaoine óga atá ag aibiú. I measc na n-ábhar a chlúdaítear tá ginmhilleadh, brúidiúlacht, an chéad phost, cúrsaí gnéis, an caidreamh idir máthair agus a híníon agus forbairt an tsaoil inmheánaigh. Léirítear na fadhbanna coitianta a bhíonn ag daoine óga agus déantar iarracht an fhírinne dhaonna a aimsiú. Ní thagann tuiscint go tapa; próiséas atá ann agus dá réir sin ní féidir an fhulaingt a sheachaint. Is féidir foghlaim ach a bheith oscailte chuige.

CQ

The Dark Beneath

Alan Gibbons
Orion, ISBN 1-84255-097-7, £4.99 (pbk)

A thriller set in a rural English village, this book tells the story of sixteen-year-old Imogen, who is being stalked by a younger boy and an older man. It covers a lot in its one hundred and eighty pages and is thought-provoking, dramatic and likely to appeal to older readers, even though some of the characters are unconvincing. Imogen's parents are overly controlling, in contradiction to their laid-back hippie quality and their interest in social and political causes; Imogen is a surprisingly passive teenager who tolerates their oppressive parenting style. Her relationship with Farid, from Afghanistan, develops quickly, and she has to weave a web of lies when he goes into hiding, helped by her. The main characters are well developed overall, and there is some beautiful use of language. Although the story is well paced, an unexpected twist in the final chapters is a little forced and weakens the overall impact of an exciting tale.

JMi

The Icarus Girl

Helen Oyeyemi
Bloomsbury, ISBN 0-7475-7548-7, £16.99 (hbk)

This extraordinary novel begins brilliantly. Jessamy is a precocious, disturbed eight-year-old, half Nigerian and half English. When the family goes on holiday to Nigeria, she finally makes a friend, the playful and amazing Tilly Tilly. Tilly Tilly turns up again when Jessamy is at home in England, and gradually it becomes clear that Tilly Tilly is not 'real' – but is she an imaginary friend, or is she some sort of ghost? Her playful antics start to turn nasty, and Jessamy's friendship with her deteriorates into desperate and dangerous possession. At this point, the novel, like Jessamy's friendship with Tilly Tilly, starts to fall apart. The action becomes tedious and the ending is forced and unsatisfying. This author has something important to say about Nigerian culture, but she hasn't yet quite worked out how to say it in novel form. With all its flaws, though, this is well worth a read, for the wonderful character of Jessamy in the first half, for its treatment of family life, for the unexpectedly tender relationship between Jessamy and her patriarchal Nigerian grandfather, and for its fascinating insight into Nigerian culture. Bright and thoughtful teenage girls will love this.

SP

(un)arranged Marriage

Bali Rai
Corgi, ISBN 0-552-54734-4, £5.99 (pbk)

This is an extraordinarily good rite-of-passage novel that tackles many of the issues besetting young British Asians. Manny's life bursts from the pages, beginning when he is thirteen and ending on his seventeenth birthday, as he makes his escape from an arranged marriage to a girl he has never met. In the intervening years he lives the universal experience of adolescence – isolation, bewilderment, raging hormones, disenchantment with his family's expectations of him. His deeply conservative father's violence has brutalised Manny's older siblings and passive mother, through his attempts to impose the dubious values of his own Punjabi childhood and culture on his British-born children. But Manny, full of hope and ambition, is determined to live his life his way. His efforts to achieve this are heartbreakingly painful and very funny. No one reading this book can fail to be lifted by its sheer exuberant optimism.

cc

Victory Street

Richard MacSween
Andersen Press, ISBN 1-84270-361-7, £5.99 (pbk)

Fifteen-year-old Ellie wants to write, but looking after her feckless mother and a younger brother with Down's syndrome seems to use up all her energy. Then, encouraged by a former English teacher, she starts to write about her Jewish neighbour's evacuation to England after the horrors of Kristallnacht. But, as Ellie visits Ruth Pearl and learns more about the brutality and anti-Semitism of the Nazi years, outside in the streets of her northern town racial tension is escalating. Ellie is forced to question her own ignorance about the racist bullying that has gone on for years, unseen or ignored by teachers and unreported by the victims – and to realise that the hatred even her older half-brother feels towards ethnic minorities and asylum-seekers has its echoes in the treatment meted out to those refugees from Nazi Germany who sought safety in a Europe that didn't always welcome them with open arms.

LM

LARRY O'LOUGHLIN

Creative Writing and Global Citizenship

Poetry Ireland's Development Education through Literature Programme encourages students to imaginatively explore global development issues through books and writing, and the different life experiences of children around the world that these reveal.

FOR YVONNE CULLEN and the boys of Scoil Plás Mhuire, Dorset Street, it's a magic fruit tree: every time the baddies cut it down, it grows back, bearing a different fruit for the child workers trapped in the nearby carpet sheds. When the children eventually escape, the tree provides a hiding-place until Suman and her colleagues from the South Asian Coalition on Child Servitude (SACCS) arrive to rescue them. In Cabra, Aislinn O'Loughlin and the girls at St Mary's School for the Deaf are exploring a story about Monica, a fatherless child lured away to the stone quarries by Boss, a local big-wig so powerful he rides an elephant. In Tralee and Limerick, students working with John W Sexton's groups are exploring child labour through the media of poetry and short stories. In Clare, Galway and Ennis, Pete Mullineaux's groups are working via theatre and song. For Nuala Lyons, in Laois and Offaly, it's fantasy, while in Dublin Séamus Cashman is combining film and poetry. In Blessington, Martina Murphy's combined primary schools groups are working through the medium of drama. Yvonne Cullen's other Dublin groups are using a combination of poetry, story and song writing. For Ger Whelan, Kate Newman, and Mark O'Sullivan, in Wexford, Cavan and Tipperary respectively, it's a journey through various prose genres.

Ten writers, working with six hundred children in seventeen different schools spread across twelve counties – the genres may vary, but the theme, broadly, will stay the same: child labour.

Writing in *Understanding Media: The Extensions Of Man*

We are no longer educating a national citizen, we are educating a global citizen, and must view issues such as environment, rights, responsibility and justice not only as they affect our local or national community but as they affect our global community

(MIT Press, 1964)[1], Canadian philosopher and writer Marshall McLuhan, perceived a world so "electronically contracted" by a century of technological advance that "…the globe is no more than a village".

McLuhan argued that as advances in technology made it possible to view events on the other side of the globe within seconds of their happening – often more quickly than we hear about events in our own communities or even families – we become increasingly aware of the global consequences of our actions. The natural corollary of that awareness is that we now have a responsibility to consider our actions in a global framework.

Forty-one years on, the world has electronically contracted to an extent far greater than perhaps than even McLuhan could have imagined.

The global village is a reality. We are the villagers, and for parents and educators this offers a real challenge. We are no longer educating a national citizen, we are educating a global citizen, and must view issues such as environment, rights, responsibility and justice not only as they affect our local or national community but as they affect our global community.

Poetry Ireland's Writers in Schools Development Education through Literature Programme is a unique response to the challenge of global citizenship education, bringing together development agencies (Trócaire, Concern, Oxfam, and SACCS) and writers in an on-going partnership that offers students the opportunity to explore development themes in a creative and participatory way, through writing and books.

In the Development Education through Literature Programme, the imagination is the essential tool

Between them, the development agencies Trócaire, Concern, Oxfam, and SACCS have more than two centuries' experience in their field. So, when experienced and talented development educators from Irish agencies – such as Trócaire's Eithne Brennan, Lizzie Noone from Concern and Suman from SACCS – combine to work in the classroom, children and teachers are taken beyond the radio sound-bite and the television image. They are facilitated to explore how real 'issues' such as poverty, civil war, debt bondage, crop failure and illiteracy affect and shape the lives of children in the developing world and in what ways these very different life experiences might be inter-related. The curriculum themes of 'just like you' and 'inter-related' offer the writers the perfect entry point to bring their particular perspectives to the project.

SYMBOLS OF SOLIDARITY AND FRIENDSHIP: HANDPRINTS OF CHILDREN FROM GRIFFEEN VALLEY EDUCATE TOGETHER NS MOUNTED ON BUTTERFLY SHAPES AND SENT TO SUMAN OF SACCS

The Development Education through Literature Programme allows the child to form and express a personal and empathic reaction to the issues broached in development education

Shortly after the publication of Philip Pullman's *Northern Lights*, author Ger Whelan was visiting a school in Wicklow. The conversation, having sailed through a number of fantasy themes, finally reached the question: 'What exactly is a daemon supposed to be?' The almost unanimous response from the class, nearly all of whom had read the book, was that the daemon represented the child's imagination. In the formal education system, particularly at second-level, the child's imagination, like the daemon, is often severed; or, if not severed, at least forced into long hibernation by the demands of the exam system.

In the Development Education through Literature Programme, the imagination is the essential tool. While the writer will talk and work with pupils on the techniques of the writing 'craft' (drafting, redrafting, character development, storyline, story-boarding, narrative structure and so on) the real creativity comes with the awakening of what Pullman calls 'the Authorial imagination' – that marvellous instrument (and here I'm paraphrasing) that allows us to pass through mountains, enter the mind of a dog, or live in a world that defies the laws of physics. The authorial imagination allows readers to enter the life of a child thousands of miles away. They can experience what it is like to be fifteen hundred kilometres away from home, working in the carpet sheds, living a life that never expands beyond the confines of the stone quarries, working as a five-year-old domestic slave or an eight-year-old child soldier.

Having received development education input from the experts, the child then uses the authorial imagination to 'experience' the information received and create a piece of work from that experience. The Development Education through Literature Programme allows the child to form and express a personal and empathic reaction to the issues broached in development education. It is this outcome that gives the programme a critical place in global citizenship education.

[1] McLuhan, Marshall, *Understanding Media: The Extensions of Man*. The MIT Press, 1994, ISBN 0262631598

LIZ PAGE

How to Choose
The IBBY Honour List and the Hans Christian Andersen Awards

The HCA Awards are the most prestigious international children's book award. Along with the IBBY Honour List, they have brought some of the best writing and illustration from nations around the world to international audiences.

ACROSS THE WORLD there are thousands of books being published for young people. We all think: *Great, it's wonderful, aren't children lucky these days?* But what are these books? How do we know which ones to choose? Which might be suitable to translate into our own language?

Since 1956, the International Board on Books for Young People – IBBY – has been trying to address this by seeking out outstanding books that are suitable for a worldwide audience. In 1956, the first international awards for children's literature, the Hans Christian Andersen Awards, were established.

The Hans Christian Andersen Awards have been known as the Little Nobel Prizes almost from the time of their inception. Every two years, each National Section of IBBY can propose two candidates, one author and one illustrator, from its country. These individuals are considered to be the best in their respective countries – authors and illustrators who have made a long-standing impact on literature for young people.

The candidates are chosen for their complete body of work, and their books and biographies are presented to the international jury. Although there are only two overall winners each time, each candidate, by being a candidate, is a winner. In 2004, there were twenty-six candidates nominated for the quality of their writing and twenty-seven candidates nominated for the quality of their illustrations: fifty-three examples of excellence in children's books; fifty-three recommendations for publishers to seek out for translations; fifty-three winners.

IBBY CONGRESS 2004, CAPE TOWN: MARTIN WADDELL RECEIVES HIS DIPLOMA FROM JEFF GARRETT, PRESIDENT OF THE HANS CHRISTIAN ANDERSEN JURY. HE WAS ALSO PRESENTED WITH THE ANDERSEN MEDAL.

When the Andersen awards were first initiated, the same jury identified single titles that were classed as outstanding, and these became the selection called the Hans Christian Andersen Honour List.

In 1974, the Honour List was split from one general category into two new categories: books honoured for their high standard of writing, and books honoured for their high standard of illustration. In 1978, a category for outstanding translations was added, to complete the trio we have today. In 1980, the selection was renamed the IBBY Honour List. From the initial 1956 selection of fifteen titles from twelve countries, the Honour List has continued to grow: the 2004 selection comprises one hundred and forty titles from forty-seven countries in thirty-seven different languages.

The selection has remained a truly international overview of publishing for young people. The IBBY Honour List is unique in that each title is chosen within its country of origin: in each category, the selectors nominate books that they feel are representative of their country at that time.

IBBY has a travelling exhibition of the Honour List books and regularly shows them to audiences around the world.

The Hans Christian Andersen Award and the Honour List bring together the diverse styles, languages and ideas, in writing and illustration for children of the countries represented. They inform international audiences about what appeals to young people in other countries and offer insight into the lives of young people there. Through these selections, we can see not only the differences between countries, but also the similarities: growing up is just as difficult whether you live in Japan, Mexico or Poland!

> *The Hans Christian Andersen Awards have been known as the Little Nobel Prizes almost from the time of their inception*

Beowulf – an Anglo-Saxon Epic

Henriette Barkow, illustrated by Alan Down
Mantra Lingua, ISBN 1-84444-0311 Somali/English, £7.50 (pbk)

There have been other retellings for children of this great Anglo-Saxon epic poem, most notably a fine one by Kevin Crossley-Holland. Unlike that version, this one sadly omits the last part of the poem, which tells of Beowulf's last stand against a dragon, his heroic death and deeply moving funeral. This seems a pity, as children – perhaps boys in particular – would enjoy that final section, in which the hero's character is most fully developed. Barkow's version is unusual in that it is dual-language, available in English and any one of eighteen other languages from Arabic to Urdu. However, the language of the English story is formal, stilted and old-fashioned, with none of the intensity or poetry of the original. The fact that the hero is a peacemaker, generously coming to the rescue of a foreign people, could have been stressed. The illustration is inspired by comic-strip and graphic-novel forms, and is effective at some points; however, the figure of Beowulf is not distinguishable from others, his face is not shown and he is not even depicted as young and strong. The relationship between text and image is rather one-dimensional, though this may be necessitated by the sheer volume of text on each page-spread.

CK

Dimo and Chewelo

Judah Seomeng, illustrated by Annabel Dunn
Pyramid Publishing, distributed by ABC*,
ISBN 99912-555-2-4, £5.95 (pbk)

This is a visually and linguistically colourful and most attractive version of a folktale from Botswana, based on an adaptation told by Samuel Seomeng to his grandchildren, who gathered at evening round campfires. As a result, the story has the immediacy and distinctive personal tone often associated with oral tradition. It contains many of the characters that inhabit Botswana's folktales – the hyena, the bush hare, and the chief protagonist and villain of this tale, Dimo, one of a tribe of giants who terrorise a peaceful, long-ago landscape in which animals and humans live and communicate harmoniously. Dimo is huge, voracious, and more brutish than cunning. It is his foolishness, as much as Mamma Chewelo's shrewdness, that leads him into the scrapes that become his downfall – and what scrapes! I cannot imagine this story or its illustrations appearing in Western primary schools, as the ending tells of local children entering and getting stuck in Dimo's anus – an unimaginable twist in a European tale for children. It takes a bird, the bebe, to peck away his flesh and enable them to escape. This rather novel parallel to the European Pied Piper of Hamelin tale is likely to offend the effete and the Freudians equally.

*African Books Collective, Oxford distributes these books in UK and Europe

MST

Here, There and Everywhere: Stories from Many Lands

Liz Weir, illustrated by Tomm Moore, The Cartoon Saloon
The O'Brien Press, ISBN 0-86278-869-2, €5.95 (pbk) [CD 0-86278-895-1, €8.95]

Consisting of nine stories from Ireland, Norway, North America and Africa – among other places – these traditional tales are told in a fresh, lively and engaging style by an accomplished and internationally known storyteller who performs all over the world. Some stories, such as 'The King with Horse's Ears', are well-known, though readers may not have been aware of how exactly the king came to acquire his ears, nor be expecting his wife's intervention on behalf of her foolish and spoilt husband – this is a new spin on a very old story. A description of how the snow came to get its colour, or the story, set long ago in Africa, of why the sky is far away, may be less familiar, at least to an Irish readership. The book is enhanced by stylised illustrations, which are both energetic and entertaining. Audience participation is encouraged by the inclusion of repetitive phrases, question-and-answer refrains and by the clapping and beating demanded in 'The Three Bears Rap', and children, at least, will respond with huge enthusiasm. The author narrates the accompanying CD, and a short theme tune and sound effects for each story help to set the mood and keep the narrative flowing.

LM

ILLUSTRATION FROM HERE, THERE AND EVERYWHERE

In The Dark

Gita Wolf and Sirish Rao, illustrated by Rathna Ramanathan
Tara Publishing, ISBN 81-86211-54-3, £9.99 (hbk)

This story will be familiar to many people: it is a much-told and much-loved traditional tale of five men who find an elephant in the dark on the way home. Each declares the elephant to be something else: the mason thinks it is a wall, the fisherman thinks it is an octopus because of its trunk, the woodcutter touches a leg and guesses it is a tree, the horseman holding the tail thinks it's a whip and the musician, feeling only the trunk, decides it is a bugle. This telling from the Sufi tradition is wonderfully wise and allows the reader or listener to enter the tale and make their own guesses along with the five men. Their debate at the end of the story is a wonderful synopsis of what has happened in this tale of wisdom for all ages. But the magic of this book also lies in its presentation. It is handcrafted and hand-calligraphed, and the letters have been pressed onto handmade paper – it even comes in its own handmade bag! Completely wonderful.

FO'S

Kwajo and the Brassman's Secret: A Tale of Old Ashanti Wisdom and Gold

Meshack Asare
Sub-Saharan Publishers, distributed by ABC, ISBN 9988-550-43-X, £6.95 (pbk)

Kwajo's days are spent helping his father to make little brass figures and his mother to prepare supper by pounding the fufu. All around him, his friends are also helping their parents, weaving kente and then printing on bright colours. When his father gives him the gift of a little brass drummer sitting on a stool, Kwajo's imagination is awakened. At the end of the day, while his friends go to the village market to play drums and dance the evening away, Kwajo dreams of finding gold and unimaginable wealth. The little drummer has magical powers and takes him on a fascinating imaginary journey to learn about greed and to gain some wisdom about the ways of men. This is an Ashanti tale, written and vividly illustrated by one of Africa's foremost storytellers. Included is a short and interesting history of the Ashanti people.

KWAJO AND THE BRASSMAN'S SECRET

CC

Pandora's Box

retold by Henriette Barkow, illustrated by Diana Mayo
Mantra Lingua, ISBN 1-85269-844-6 Greek/English, £7.50 (pbk)

Zeus, the king of the gods, sent Prometheus and Epimetheus to create creatures to live on the earth. Prometheus stole fire from the gods and taught man to use it. Furious, Zeus punished Prometheus and planned revenge on man by creating Pandora, to whom he gave many gifts – including that of curiosity. On the wedding day of Epimetheus and Pandora, Zeus gave them a box that was never to be opened. Eventually Pandora, driven by her curiosity, opened the box and unleashed 'hate and greed, pestilence and disease' on man's hitherto perfect world. Fortunately, hope was also released. As both an introduction to ancient civilisations and an exploration of world creation stories, this book has a definite place on library, school and home bookshelves. Also available in dual-language editions, in English with Albanian, Arabic, Bengali, Chinese, Czech, Farsi, French, German, Gujarati, Italian, Panjabi, Polish, Portuguese, Serbo-Croat, Somali, Spanish, Tamil, Turkish, Urdu or Vietnamese.

RH

Tales from the West Indies

Philip Sherlock
Oxford University Press, ISBN 0-19-275077-1, £4.99 (pbk)

The late Philip Sherlock, an educationalist, historian, poet and writer for children, spent a long and fruitful lifetime engaged in the cultural revival of his beloved Jamaica. The stories in this collection include those of the Carib and Arawak peoples native to the Caribbean and America – tales that, for the most part, explain the beginnings of things – and stories of West African origin featuring the favourite trickster and original Spiderman, Anansi. It is a truly cross-cultural collection, in which the people of the West Indies have made their own of tales from very different parts of the world. The language is finely controlled, simple but moving. Brutality and cruelty are not ignored. Superbly written, each tale is dramatic, full of tension, surprise and humour. Each character is vividly realised, while the landscape explodes into life. The book has not dated since its first publication in 1966, under the title *West Indian Folk Tales*; it has been in print, and deservedly so, almost consistently ever since. It is as fresh as ever, the work of a poet. Unfortunately, for some reason, OUP did not publish it with Joan Kiddell Monroe's vibrant and striking illustrations , which so captured the spirit and energy of the stories in the earlier editions. The illustrations in this edition are dull, lifeless, even unclear, and add nothing.

CK

Tenzin's Deer: A Tibetan Tale

Barbara Soros, illustrated by Danuta Mayer
Barefoot Books, ISBN 1-84148-809-7, £10.99 (hbk)

A gentle book that, depending on the age of the reader, can be read on many different levels. Tenzin, a young boy, finds a wounded deer and nurses her back to health, but eventually he must release the deer back into the wild and cope with the loss of his relationship with the animal. This book is about losing what each of us loves enough to let go; on another level, it is about compassion and the healing power of love that lies within each of us. It provides a glimpse into a culture where a young boy can hold the wisdom of many generations in his memory, a culture that recognises that difficult lessons must be learned on the path to enlightenment. The combination of warm and detailed illustrations with a simply told yet profound narrative makes this book quite special.

FO'S

The Barber's Clever Wife

Narinder Dhami, illustrated by Katja Bundlow
A&C Black, ISBN 0-7136-6860-1, £4.99 (pbk)

This is a rather intriguing story set in a Punjabi valley village near the Himalayan mountains. The central character is Ruby, whose husband Bulbul is a lazy, incompetent barber who would prefer to sleep or even beg rather than work. Ruby is a resourceful survivor who figures out a scheme to make money. When they become rich, she outwits a gang of thieves who try to steal all their money. From a Western perspective, the tale appears rather sexist – particularly the conclusion; however, it also offers an opportunity to explore culturally different values and gender roles. A range of messages may be discerned in this tale – for example, that a woman can be effective and may achieve success through cunning rather than power. There is also a universal message: if you find yourself married to a good-for-nothing, don't despair! The text is illustrated throughout with simple, quirky, monotone drawings, which will help to engage young readers. It is an attractive story and would work well read aloud to under-sevens, or as a page-turning read-it-yourself. Adults can use this story to explore children's understanding of stereotypes. Children will undoubtedly ask their own questions and express their own views.

AO'D

The Children of Lir – A Celtic Legend

retold by Dawn Casey, illustrated by Diana Mayo
Mantra Lingua, ISBN 1-85269-818-7 Irish/English, £7.50 (pbk)

It is wonderful to have a colourful bilingual version of this old Irish legend and heartening to see that it is also available in twenty other languages, in each case along with English. However, the execution is not quite as splendid as the idea. The English text is generally presented in a lyrical, 'high' mythic style – with plenty of words like 'upon', 'wondrous' and 'brow' – but there is a little unevenness in the pacing of the story. The Irish translation also adopts a lyrical, quasi-oral style, good for reading aloud, but the rather elevated register is unlikely to be accessible to most child-readers. Moreover, there are many variant (non-standard) spellings and several proofreading errors, notably in the punctuation, both of which are likely to cause confusion. Bíonn fírinní uilíocha faoi chúrsaí na beatha i scéalta béaloidis, de ghnáth, pé cultúr as a dtagann siad. Ní haon ionadh é mar sin gur breá le léitheoirí óga iad. Is deas é ceann de mhórscéalta na Gaeilge a bheith á chur i láthair anseo. Scéal an-tarraingteach é *Clann Lir* agus is aoibhinn iad na pictiúir a mhaisíonn é sa leabhar seo, go háirithe iad siúd a bhfuil ealaí iontu. Is é an trua é nach bhfuil an scil chéanna ag an ealaíontóir seo agus í i mbun aghaidheanna: tá cuid de na pictiúir garbh go leor. Rud eile: níl aon uimhreacha ar na leathanaigh, agus is mór an crá é sin, sa seomra ranga ach go háirithe.

SP

REVIEWS: FOLKTALES, MYTH AND LEGEND

The Mahabharatha, Part 1 – A Child's View

Samhita Arni
Tara Publishing, ISBN 81-86211-70-5, £9.99 (hbk)

This is a bold and clever retelling of an ancient Indian myth, selected by the author 'because it is so evil' and interspersed with comment and opinion by an extraordinary young writer. The myth is complex and robust and makes one wonder how the ancient myths and legends become the preserve of children, and young children at that. All human life really is here – the king draws his sperm, puts it on a leaf, and summons a swallow to carry the leaf to his queen. The sperm falls into the sea and is eaten by a fish, which is caught by a fisherman who finds a beautiful baby girl in its belly. He and his wife, being childless, adopt the baby, who inevitably grows into a beautiful maiden. Themes common to most folktales appear here: the special significance of particular numbers, the childless royals, the younger woman and the older man, and the mating of gods and mortals. Yet this is not an easy read for the uninitiated. The names are strange to the Western eye and ear, and the myth is peopled with throngs of characters whose adventures are not always easy to follow. However, for anyone willing to make a little effort, this is a wonderful place to learn about Indian mythology.

IB

The Story of the Crow and the Frog

Walter Bgoya, illustrated by Christine Steinberg-Mund
Mkuki na Nyota Publishers, distributed by ABC,
ISBN 9987-686-41-9, £7.99 (pbk)

This is an interesting short tale that, like one of Aesop's fables, conveys a message. Its main moral is that might is not always right, and that respect should be shown for all efforts, no matter how small, and for all individuals, no matter how different from oneself. One other message is that the young can be wise and can teach their elders, a point that will be particularly appreciated by young readers. The story tells of a competition between a large crow and an old frog to see which can travel the fastest. Before the race begins, a council of frogs is called, and a young female has a plan that will confuse the crow and ultimately allow the old frog to be seen to win. In the end both frog and crow respect each other, and the reader is left with the secret of the frog's success. The text is supported by attractive pastel-like illustrations. It is not clear where the story is set, but the trees and lush vegetation convey a tropical feel.

GO'C

The Seven Wise Princesses

Wafa' Tarnowska, illustrated by Nilesh Mistry
Barefoot Books, ISBN 1-84148-021-5, £14.99 (hbk)

This is an extraordinarily beautiful prose retelling of a Sufi poet's twelfth-century epic poem 'Haft Paykar'.' The story weaves the complex and beautifully written tale of Bahram, Shah of Persia. He finds within his palace a room with seven portraits of princesses from India, Greece, Arabia, Russia, Morocco, China and Persia, and he builds a pavilion for each princess, each decorated in a particular colour and corresponding to one of the planets. Each princess dresses in the colour of her pavilion and has a tale linked to her chosen colour. Over seven days, Bahram visits each princess and listens to her story. The stories are designed to teach him about truth, patience, perseverance, forgiveness, humility, wisdom and love so he can become a great ruler. But each story also incorporates the culture of its narrator princess, making the whole a rich and varied tapestry of story, warmly and vividly told and designed for reading aloud. Copious notes are provided to give background and explanation. But it is the quite stunning illustrations accompanying the narrative that contain the real magic and give an insight into this ancient and wonderful epic.

FO'S

The Story Tree – Tales to Read Aloud

retold by Hugh Lupton, illustrated by Sophie Fatus
Barefoot Books, ISBN 1-84148-311-7, £12.99 (hbk)

'Delight' is the only word that comes to mind when reading this collection of well-known and less familiar stories. Hugh Lupton has collected and presented quite a range of traditional stories from Germany, India, Russia, Norway, England and the African-American and Jewish traditions. These stories are skilfully retold, with the emphasis on wonderful language and the engagement of the audience in the narrative. The illustrations are quirky but truly delightful, catching the essence of each story and drawing the reader into the narrative. The collection is well conceived and the stories very accessible as read-alouds for a young audience.

FO'S

The Tiger and the Jackal: a Traditional Indian Tale

retold by Vivian French, illustrated by Alison Bartlett
Walker Books, ISBN 0-7445-6878-1, £2.99 (pbk)

This is a beautifully illustrated retelling of a traditional tale, published by Walker Books as part of its 'Reading Together' series aimed at early readers. Through vivid illustration and constant repetition, it recounts the story of an untrustworthy tiger, a little boy and a wily jackal. Although rather too difficult for the inexperienced reader, it will certainly appeal to even the youngest listener. The moral of the story, about keeping promises, is one that will be readily accessible to the young listener or reader, and the cultural references are clearly conveyed through the illustrations. The text itself is visually attractive and is specifically aimed at parents who want to introduce their child to reading. As an added resource, there are helpful ideas, specifically aimed at parents, at the front and back of the text. An attractive little book that does exactly what it says on the tin.

JO'H

The Three Birds from Olongo

retold by Agbo and Margaret Folarin, illustrated by Agbo Folarin
Spectrum Books, distributed by ABC, ISBN 978-029-332-9, £4.95 (pbk)

This simple retelling of a Yoruba folktale follows the plight of the birds of Olongo, who are faced with a terrible drought. Three of the birds must travel to the land of men to learn about farming, and they hope to return with new skills that will save Olongo, 'the most exciting and most beautiful country you can possibly imagine'. However, they soon discover that this new knowledge comes at a price. Drawing upon oral traditions of West Africa, the fable documents the necessity of resilience and resourcefulness in a time of crisis, but also the sacrifices that can result from attempting to meet certain goals. Agbo and Margaret Folarin's narration retains the oral nature of the folktale in the retelling, primarily through the use of long sentences, with the story realised to its full potential when read aloud. Agbo Folarin's colourful illustrations of birds of all shapes and sizes make a significant contribution to the creation of a fantasy world. However, the quality of reproduction is often poor, while the borders surrounding the illustrations lack consistency of form.

THE THREE BIRDS OF OLONGO

PW

The Village of Round and Square Houses

Ann Grifalconi
Macmillan, ISBN 0-333-48521-1, £4.99 (pbk)

This sensitively retold story from the village of Tos in Cameroon, West Africa, is atmospheric in both the text and the beautiful pastel illustrations. A young girl, homesick for her native place, relates how the men have ended up living in square houses and the women in round ones. The gentle existence of the village, with its daily rituals of eating and preparing food, provides an excellent introduction to another way of life. The legend itself is told by the young girl's grandmother in a poetic style, the rhythm of the words adding to the almost mesmerising illustration. The traumatic aftermath of the eruption of the volcano is particularly striking: the lavish colour of the preceding pages becomes almost monochrome, only to gradually regain colour as the villagers rebuild their huts and reclaim the land. The resilience of the villagers, and their close affinity with nature and the land, demonstrate a strength that will appeal to all ages from eight up.

THE VILLAGE OF ROUND AND SQUARE HOUSES

JD

The Winter King and the Summer Queen

Mary Lister, illustrated by Diana Mayo
Barefoot Books, ISBN 1-84148-356-7, £9.99 (hbk)

This book for newly independent readers very much reflects the author's background as a storyteller. The narrative is set in two contrasting kingdoms: Queen Goldenlight rules over the Land of Flaming Sun, while King Icicle rules the Land of Icy Darkness. Each has a court reflecting his or her kingdom, so the queen's is peopled by happy courtiers who send light and warmth to the earth, while the king's court contains gloomy people who like nothing better than to direct icestorms and rain at the earth. The story highlights the age-old battle between good and evil, light and dark, and the author avoids any sense of benevolence within the darker kingdom, so the resolution – a bridge between the worlds forming in the shape of a rainbow – really works. However, the names of some of the courtiers ('Sunshine Sally', 'Callum Cloud' or 'Maya Monsoon') seem a little forced, and, though a good oral storytelling device, this does not necessarily work in the written narrative.

FO'S

Tibetan Tales for Little Buddhas

Naomi C Rose
Clear Light Publishing, ISBN 1-57416-081-8, $16.95 (hbk)

The three stories in this bilingual book for young readers depict life in the 'land of snows' among the tallest mountains in the world. The text, in English and Tibetan with its strikingly pretty alphabet, reveals different kinds of learning based on Tibetan Buddhism. The first concerns our attitude to the future: through a series of incidents, Yeshi learns to be at peace with how life goes. The second tells of orphaned Jomo, who must work hard cleaning the house and shepherding yaks. She is afraid of her Aunt Peta, but learns to see humanity in the face of fear. The third story is about Chunda, a boy monk who injures his ankle and, while alone in the wild sleeping with the goats, encounters a Yeti and becomes more self-aware and wise. The author immersed herself in Tibetan culture for many years; her illustrations offer an authentic glimpse of a very different way of life, and there is an unusual light, with skies of many shades. There is some information about Tibet and a foreword by the Dalai Lama, who writes, 'Because the stories are set in Tibet, readers in other lands will naturally become aware of the existence of our country and of the values we hold dear.'

AO'D

Performance Literacy
Storytelling With and Without Books

Storyteller Brett Dillingham illustrates how encouraging children to write and perform their own stories can promote literacy in environments where access to books is rare.

LAST WEEK I visited a Yupik Eskimo village to teach performance literacy, in which children write and tell their own stories. The village library was in poor shape – outdated books, near-empty shelves and few books that were interesting or culturally relevant to the community. It was a typical library in an Alaskan village, typical of high poverty urban schools in the United States, typical of high poverty communities worldwide.

How do we foster useful and motivating reading experiences for children who live in these book-scarce environments?

One way is to encourage performance literacy. Start by telling children a story. Make the storytelling itself interesting by integrating facial expressions, sound – sound effects, rhythm, intonation – and body movement. Seeing a story picture painted this way, children willingly suspend their disbelief. They sit transfixed, creating pictures and events in their minds.

Because their access to interesting, relevant print is limited, these children need to craft their own stories, not just receive the ones that a teacher or storyteller performs. They need to be encouraged to write and tell their own stories. I present them with a subject that is culturally relevant to the students and community. The children brainstorm different problems and solutions, or conflicts and resolutions, to choose from, and write them on the board. Once they have all chosen and written down their subjects, problems and solutions, I ask them to tell and re-tell their stories to one another in pairs. They do this before most have written the first drafts of their stories. This is

INUPIAK STUDENT PRACTISING MAKING FACIAL EXPRESSIONS FOR STORYTELLING IN ALASKA

important because so many children have a hard time putting the ideas in their heads onto paper in story format; if they have already verbalised their ideas in story format, the writing is much easier.

When they have told their 'draft' stories, they continue writing. The children are encouraged to draw pictures that help them remember their stories. When they have written their stories and practised in front of the class, they can then tell their stories to an audience – their parents, a class next door, a group at a library or in a hospital, anywhere they can 'publish' their work.

THE STORYTELLING/READING CONNECTION

Reading is one component of literacy; speaking, listening, and writing are the others. These components are interrelated and support one another. For example, when children write, they are reading; when they read, they see words they have heard in new sentence structures; they learn new vocabulary from reading.

Once students have written and told their own stories, listened to their classmates tell their stories, and 'published' their stories to other classes or audiences, they have immersed themselves in all aspects of literacy. They have

INUPIAK STUDENTS LISTENING TO AND LAUGHING DURING STORYTELLING IN ALASKA

written their own stories and read them many times. They have listened to their classmates' stories and re-told them. Performance literacy provides the tools and the motivation to write, read, tell and listen to more stories.

Stories make us hungry for more words. It's re-assuring to know we can feed our appetites and create stories of our own, even when we, sadly, lack access to good books.

How do we foster useful and motivating reading experiences for children who live in these book-scarce environments?

MATT MCDANIEL

The Akha Book Project, Thailand

The Akha Book Project has helped to document the Akha language and to preserve the culture and community of the Akha people in the face of many obstacles.

THE AKHA HILL TRIBE PEOPLE, numbering approximately four hundred thousand, live in northern Thailand, Burma, Laos and China. They live by an oral tradition and have no record of an historical script. Although several overlapping scripts developed through years of missionary work with the Akha people, these missionary efforts did not sufficiently preserve the Akha culture and history. In fact, the mission scripts were sometimes inaccurate and difficult to use. A concise and simple phonetic system of writing was needed.

In 1991, the Akha Book Project was started in Thailand by the Akha Heritage Foundation. After seven years of meetings with numerous Akha writers – many of them traditional Akha and some of them Akha who had worked with missionary groups – a new script, using letters from the Roman alphabet, was ninety-eight per cent completed.

In 1991, the Akha Book Project was started in Thailand by the Akha Heritage Foundation

The Akha Book Project then began producing books, written in this script, by and about the Akha people. After a number of years we had published a book on culture, a handbook of words and a children's alphabet book. A children's work-book is also under production at this time, along with more books on Akha culture. In addition, we began publishing the *Akha Journal of the Golden Triangle* – a book intended to inform the wider public about the situation of the Akha people – in English, Thai and Akha, combining all three languages together in one book.

To date, the Akha Book Project has distributed seven thousand journals, twenty thousand alphabet books and limited numbers of books on Akha culture. Some of the children's books have also been used in classes for children in Akha villages. One of our recent milestones was the purchase of a printing press, which will allow us to move forward with the publication of more Akha-language books. These books will also go to Akha who are in prison.

To date, the Akha Book Project has distributed seven thousand journals, twenty thousand alphabet books and limited numbers of books on Akha culture

While working on the Akha Book Project, we discerned a number of obstacles to our work. Literacy for the Akha people and the use of Akha language did not have widespread support from the national governments in the countries they inhabit. The influence of missionary work in Akha areas was often counter-productive to the preservation of the Akha language and culture. The Akha Project also found that the Akha people's ability to support their communities was being eroded by some missionary and governmental activities. In this atmosphere, any effort on our part to increase literacy, and protect the culture, history and language of the Akha people has to be combined with an all-out effort to protect their human rights as well.

This is and continues to be our dual goal: preservation of the Akha language, as inseparable from the preservation of the Akha people. Without support for Akha people, their unique language and culture will also wither and die.

Some books can be seen in the downloads section of www.akha.org

All the Colours of the Earth

edited by Wendy Cooling, illustrated by Sheila Moxley
Frances Lincoln, ISBN 1-84507-014-3, £12.99 (hbk)

In the introduction, editor Wendy Cooling says, 'These poems are about seeing ourselves not just as members of a street, village or city community, but as citizens of the world.' She has brought together some of her favourite poems from different countries and traditions in this attractive hardback. All kinds of human experiences are chronicled in this thought-provoking collection. Here is a poem from Felice Holman in the United States about being lost among supermarket shelves, one from Joan Poulson in the voice of a British child who can't imagine how her friend's granny lives in a village in India, a jaunty Jamaican/US poem 'Fruits' by Opal Palmer Adisa, a skipping rope song from Trinidad, and a moving ode to children who work in dumps in Nicaragua by Gloria Guevara. The illustrations are outstanding. Moxley uses a rich palette of deep purples, lush greens, striking reds and oranges, her children are full of character and she captures the mood of each poem perfectly. Highly recommended for home, classroom and library.

SW

Alphabets are Amazing Animals

Anushka Ravishankar, illustrated by Christiane Pieper
Tara Publishing, ISBN 81-86211-72-1, £7.99 (hbk)

A sophisticated, imaginative alphabet book full of surprises for anyone jaded with more conventional alphabet books, this is a real winner. A double-page spread is devoted to each letter of the alphabet and the creature illustrating it. Alliterative sentences offer descriptions of creatures, some familiar, others unusual, like the 'Untidy uakaris'. Most are ridiculous and full of fun, often forming tongue-twisters. Try saying 'Quick quails queue quietly' quickly, or gallop along with 'Gloomy geese gobble grey gum'. Even 'Vipers visit vultures' is a challenge. The artwork is stylised and bold, slightly in the style of Dr Seuss – and, indeed, Seuss lovers will adore this mixture of wordplay and zany illustration. Each spread is illustrated in one flat colour, and each creature is described by one adjective, giving opportunities for learning beyond ABC.

VC

Anything But A Grabooberry

Anushka Ravishankar, illustrated by Rathan Ramanathan
Tara Publishing, ISBN 81-86211-43-8, £9.99 (hbk)

This is a most unusual book. The text is pretty straight-forward – a nonsense verse, 'I want to be a …' repeated several times and always ending with '… anything but a grabooberry.' The rhythm and sense of each sentence attracts the reader – but the magic of this book is that the words themselves provide the illustrations to accompany each sentence. This 'type-play' is done in a variety of ways: letters of a word are positioned to make the shape of the object, visual hints are incorporated into letter strings, or letters are decorated to denote an object. The reader is enticed into suspending normal reading patterns to spend time lingering over each sentence, relishing the humour and genius of the hidden illustrations. A book to be shared with readers of six and up, as well as a book to be read alone.

FO'S

Clotty Malotty and All Her Friends: A Collection of Rhymes with Artwork

written by children from Finglas, County Dublin, Ireland
Kids' Own Publishing Partnership, ISBN 1-902432-19-3, €10 (pbk)

These rhymes, collected by primary-school children in Finglas, include several that allude directly to the Traveller community. Some use cant, the particular language of that community, and others would be familiar to anyone brought up in an English-speaking community. The assimilation of ideas – some in parodied rhymes ('Hail Mary, / Full of grace / Hitch up the ass / And go to Naas'), some by adaptation of rhymes to Traveller culture – is paralleled in the illustrations, which are photographs of plasticine configurations of the rhymes, raw material pulled into an approximation of a particular form. Vibrant and attractive, this juxtaposition of rhyme and representation, of familiar and less familiar, is at once a refreshing resource for new rhymes and an archive of rhymes otherwise likely to be lost from the largely oral culture of the Traveller community.

AP

A collection of rhymes with artwork by children from Finglas, County Dublin, Ireland

Excuse Me, Is this India?

Anushka Ravishankar, illustrated by Anita Leutwiler
Tara Publishing, ISBN 81-86211-56-X, £7.99 (hbk)

Told in the form of an extended poem, *Excuse Me, Is this India?* is a wonderfully entertaining story, enhanced greatly by Anita Leutwiler's intricate, colourful illustrations. When Aunt Anna returns from India, she brings home lots of stories, as well as the gift of a quilt that depicts all the wonderful things she's seen on her visit: elephants, bandicoots and the like. The narrator falls asleep under the quilt and drifts into a sleep filled with dreams of exotic and wonderful scenes from life in India – people, three-wheeled cars, lost bandicoots, temples, airports and planes. The only sad part about dreaming is waking up, as the narrator discovers! This is a fun and slightly absurd story. The text is large and easy to read, and the intense accompanying illustrations and panels will encourage very young readers to generate tales and verse of their own.

MNiDh

From Mouth to Mouth: Oral Poems from around the World

edited by John Agard and Grace Nichols, illustrated by Annabel Wright
Walker Books, ISBN 0-7445-8383-7, £5.99 (pbk)

This book presents mainly great oral verse that has tripped from tongues worldwide. It is a pleasure to see familiar rhymes placed beside unaccustomed African-American, African and even Eastern and antipodean verse. The introduction entreats readers to enter the world of oral verse, to take seriously the possibility that 'a word spoken by chance might have serious consequences'. While this emphasis is admirable, the book nonetheless inserts itself into a *written*, even scholarly tradition, as the acknowledgements indicate. I found myself constantly wanting to know more about these poems. Why were these versions chosen, and not others? Why are some translators identified, and not others? Why are some, but not all, poems given in the original? And if a poem is in its original language, why not its title also? A category such as 'Australian' or 'African' is hardly helpful, given the diversity of these continents' cultures. An interesting and useful collection of poems, this book would have benefited from the scholarly apparatus that would help readers.

MST

Fruits: A Caribbean Counting Poem

Valerie Bloom, illustrated by David Axtell
Macmillan, ISBN 0-333-65312-2, £5.99 (pbk)

Twelve verses describe how one little girl samples ten different Caribbean fruits in one day. Each verse is accompanied by a full-page painting in an 'oil-on-board' effect, softly realistic, catching the mood of the unfolding story. The sunshiny feel of its location spills out from the pages, matching the words, which catch the rhythm and intonation of Caribbean speech while remaining entirely intelligible to a non-Caribbean audience. The temptations the young speaker meets demand to be read aloud: 'Three sweet-sop, well I jus' might / Give one o' them a nice big bite.' There is a glossary explaining what the fruits are like. A lovely bedtime book.

VC

One River Many Creeks: Poems from All Around the World

edited by Valerie Bloom
Macmillan, ISBN 0-330-39768-0, £4.99 (pbk)

These hundred-odd poems from a multiplicity of cultures include work by internationally familiar names (Yeats, Whitman, Walcott, Tagore, Ritsos, Heaney), by many (in translation) less familiar to English speakers, and some folk verse. Multicultural in intent and scope, the collection makes a simple introduction for young readers and teachers to the worldwide poetic treasure of ideas, words, rhythms, textures and styles. Much of the content is light, where I might have hoped for more depth and quality; but light and easy is very often a valid route into poetry for many. There is an apparent lack of meaningful structure – rivers and creeks make very identifiable tracks, and less spread of place might have allowed for more intriguing currents. The book is too intent on one from everywhere, *pace* the subtitle.

SC

One, Two, Tree!

Anushka Ravishankar, Sirish Rao and Durga Bai
Tara Publishing, ISBN 81-86211-80-2, £8.99 (hbk)

Here is a beautifully produced counting book in which numbers are shown as digits and words. The generously sized pages are spacious and clean – this is a model of good design. Alternate double-page spreads show a number and an insect, reptile or animal attached to the number; the next spread then has a rhyme about the creature – for example, six is illustrated by 'six fussy pigs decid[ing] to leave their sty'. These rhymes accumulate, as all of the creatures shown perch in a broad-branched tree, until 'Nine drowsy cows squeeze in and start to snore', followed by 'Ten hefty elephants … is there room for more?' Durga Bai, the artist, is a member of the Gond tribe in central India, and we are told that her work here is typical Gond painting. It is stylised and intricate, but could be imitated by children, giving this book a much broader application than just teaching numbers. But, while it has many pedagogical virtues, buy it for its aesthetic virtues – it is also excellent financial value.

VC

The Skipping Rope Snake

Carol Ann Duffy, illustrated by Lydia Monks
Macmillan, ISBN 0-333-99327-6, £4.99 (pbk)

Award-winning poet Carol Ann Duffy is the author of many collections of poems for both adults and children. Here she collaborates with illustrator Lydia Monks. In this book, a jungle snake finds itself used as a skipping rope by a little girl when her games with other jungle animals are not so successful. The bold, colourful illustrations with paint and cut-out textures and patterns give a delightful jungle feel to this book, and the rhymes work their way through the jungle to bedtime. Although Duffy is the better known of this partnership, the illustrations here are more successful than the text, which is somewhat slight. Full of decorative detail, this jungle is full of little insects and big animals.

JFi

Tiger on a Tree

Anushka Ravishankar, illustrated by Pulak Biswas
Tara Publishing, ISBN 81-86211-35-7, £9.99 (hbk)

This picture book, which won the Biennale of Illustrations in Bratislava, immediately stands out from the crowd. The cover and inner pages are of rough handmade paper and the illustrations, boldly executed in orange, black and cream, are bright and eye-catching. The story of a tiger's adventures in his native land is simple, but the way in which the text and the illustrations work together is truly breathtaking. The little tiger's curiosity is contagious, propelling the reader through the book. Every page layout is different, and the positioning of the text mirrors the movement of the tiger. When the tiger is swimming, the words flow across the page like waves, when he is chasing other animals they run from top to bottom, and when he himself is being chased they run from bottom to top, graphically conveying his reversal of fortune. The theme of interdependence is beautifully expressed, and subtly complemented by the balance between black and cream in the text. With its dramatic page-turning surprises and onomatopoeic rhymes, this little book will surely be read over and over again.

LMy

Today is My Day

Anushka Ravishankar, illustrated by Piet Grobler
Tara Publishing, ISBN 81-86211-76-4, £7.99 (hbk)

The young female narrator in this picture book told in rhyme is having a 'me' day, and anyone who makes demands on her comes to a sticky but appropriate end. Her father flaps at her and is turned into a bird. Her mother sings her a lullaby and ends up trapped in the telly. The text is clever and engaging, in a Belloc-meets-Dr-Seuss way. Unusually, the type is mainly in red, with some black, and is interspersed with large block capitals where emphasis is required. The stylish illustration is also in red and black, with blocks of ochre. A combination of techniques is used to good effect: detailed line drawing, with scraffito and charcoal providing texture and depth and solid blocks of colour adding contrast. No strong sense of time or place is obvious, though the darker skin tones and black hair of the stylised characters might suggest Asia. Altogether an amusing and engaging book for readers aged seven and up.

IB

Under the Moon and Over the Sea: a Collection of Caribbean Poems

edited by John Agard and Grace Nichols, illustrated by Cathie Felstead, Jane Ray, Christopher Corr, Satoshi Kitamura and Sara Fanelli
Walker Books, ISBN 0-7445-8942-7, £8.99 (pbk)

This book's good fortune is great editors and illustrators. It's a happy marriage of shimmering tropical colour, rap rhythms, folksy wisdom and joie de vivre. Its poems are as scintillating and phosphorescent as the pages. Familiar poets joust with the less well known. Although the anthology is organised thematically, a strand woven throughout the magic carpet is the movement between Britain and the Caribbean. This book brings the Caribbean to the chilly British Isles, but not as an exotic holiday resort – it is historicised rather than romanticised. And yet, Caribbean character is retained: Faustin Charles's poem has a wonderful line in otherworldly, terrifying creatures; Telcine Turner's 'Listen' is sensuous, and the anonymous 'Banyan Tree' combines a reggae idiom with exotic imagery. This book has all kinds of treasures to be shared and savoured.

MST

Whoop an' Shout

Valerie Bloom, illustrated by David Dean
Macmillan, ISBN 0-330-41580-8, £4.99 (pbk)

A Jamaica-born perform-ance poet, Valerie Bloom brings delightful joy, wit, intelligence and craft to this volume of fifty poems. Being a malaria victim, I loved 'A Mosquito'; and, being terri-fied of shellfish, I will quote 'Seafood's Off' with glee at the next dinner party. 'The Moon is a Starfish', 'Omen', 'I Heard', and the 'Carnival Queen' are brimful of truths

and joys; 'The Whooping Boys' is a vast landscape in three wonderful octets – poem after poem here is alight with spirit and story, fun and discovery. She also slips in some pieces such as 'A Nonet' and 'Rondel' as aids to the craft of poem-making. There is a glossary to help readers enter the Caribbean idiom and atmosphere – though, in truth, a reading aloud will suffice most of the time. Terrific – even if you are only interested in the cultural impact of a 'Computer Virus'. This poet clearly loves children (and teaching) and brings sunshine and sport to her craft. Bloom draws wonderfully on her Caribbean background, not only for subject matter but for language, rhythm and atmos-phere, and she shapes her experiences on this side of the Atlantic through that culture.

SC

KEN McCUE

Chinese Brought to Book in New Intercultural Academy

The Irish-Chinese Arts, Cultural and Shaolin Academy will be an important addition to the development of Chinese arts, heritage and language in Ireland. Ken McCue details some of the programmes that it will undertake.

OVER FORTY-FIVE THOUSAND Chinese-speaking people (Mandarin and Cantonese) live in the Irish Republic, yet there is little public evidence of their rich cultural heritage. Events like the Dublin Chinese New Year Festival, and the programme of Chinese Arts and Culture in Ireland launched in 2004 by the Department of Arts, Sports and Tourism, have brought about some recognition of Chinese culture in Ireland, but there is still a long way to go. Without the means to engage in intercultural dialogue, many of our new citizens will remain isolated. The rapid changes in Irish society have led to bias and to some racist incidents. Much more is needed, from both state and municipal agencies, to support this large ethnic group in creating a cultural imprint in their host country.

Support groups like the Chinese Society of Ireland and the Irish Chinese Information Centre, along with friendship societies such as Irish Chinese Association and the Irish Chinese Cultural Society, have made attempts to promote Chinese language and culture among the Irish-Chinese and Irish population, through education programmes and seminars. The private company Asian Institute has also made a major contribution by introducing Chinese customs to the Irish business community. A new umbrella organisation, the Irish-Chinese Arts, Cultural and Shaolin Academy, will comprehensively address the issues around cultural integration and will have an immense impact in terms of the generation of social capital and the ongoing development of a more intercultural society on this island.

The Academy is in the process of establishing an intercultural centre in Dublin city centre. This facility is modelled on Liverpool's successful Pagoda of Hundred Harmony, which houses many arts, cultural and heritage groups in the oldest Chinatown in Europe.

Much more is needed to support this large ethnic group in creating a cultural imprint in their host country

The new Dublin resource centre will include a library with public access, and an education centre that will promote the teaching of Chinese languages and culture in Irish schools. Furthermore, the Education Research Department of the Academy will encourage the public library services to stock Chinese-language books.

The largest local authority in the Irish Republic, Dublin City Council – with an estimated population of twenty thousand Chinese people in its catchment area – through education programmes and seminars already has a number of Chinese-language books in its Dublin Central Library at the ILAC Centre. Of the twenty-one Chinese books on its shelves, one is a translation of the complete lyrical poems of W.B. Yeats, printed on newsprint, translated by Fu Hao and published by the Chinese Workers' Press in 1994. This book is a good example of what can be achieved on a shoestring and is a good shelf companion to the translation of Joyce's *Ulysses* by the Chinese academic Jin Di, who was recently honoured at the Irish Writers' Centre. The Chester Beatty Library, located at Dublin Castle, has a wonderful collection of literature from the Orient, with many jade-covered books on permanent display. Pending the installation of the new library, the fledgling Academy has a temporary arrangement with the BaiYa Centre at 179 Parnell Street, Dublin 1, where popular journals and magazines in Chinese are made available to the general public.

The new Dublin resource centre will include a library with public access, and an education centre that will promote the teaching of Chinese languages and culture in Irish schools

In the meantime, the representatives of the Academy will be entering into discussions with the Asia-Europe Foundation and the United Nations Education, Scientific and Cultural Organisation (UNESCO) about the development of the new library and educational resource centre. It is hoped that international pressure will encourage the Arts Council, government departments and local authorities to adopt European and international directives in this area, and thus further the process of making Chinese culture available to a wide community.

A Beggar in Paradise: Living with the Inca Indians

Chris Conroy
Mentor Press, ISBN 0-947548-92-0, €16.50 (pbk)

Carmelite priest Chris Conroy spent fifteen years living with the Inca Indians in the Andes of Peru. Here he found the descendants of the once-proud Inca civilisation reduced to abject poverty, a despised minority in their own land. Accepting their poverty as his own, 'Papay Christobal' adapted to the ways of the Indians. He learned to return their warm 'big hugs' and, if he was not to go hungry, to accept whatever came out of 'the big brown pot', even when it looked remarkably like guinea pig. He coped with the hostility of Spanish estate owners and police, who were often suspicious of any 'friend of the Indians'. Conroy tells the history of Peru with understanding and describes its ruins with awe, but his empathy with the Indians brings the book to life. He understands the innate spirituality of these forgotten people and ministers to this. It doesn't matter to him that they are as untruthful to God as they are to him, because he accepts that, for them, the truth is what you want to hear. Forget about the 'paradise' – read this book for the 'beggars' and for a very wonderful priest.

AF

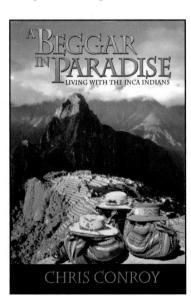

All Kinds of Beliefs

Emma Damon, paper engineering by Richard Ferguson
Mantra Lingua, ISBN 1-84444-163-6 Somali/English, £9.99 (hbk)

Young children will enjoy this novelty book, which effectively explores the external aspects of religious belief – dress, places of worship, festivals – rather than the beliefs themselves. Human similarities beneath the exterior are emphasised, especially on the page where flaps may be lifted to show the same face wearing different headdresses. A Christian girl is shown wearing a First Communion headdress, but when the flap is turned, the same face becomes that of a Muslim girl wearing a *hijaab* over her hair. The book has very little text, leaving some words unexplained, which encourages questions and further reading. This book, available in four other dual-language editions (English with Arabic, Bengali, Chinese or Urdu), is an ideal, colourful if simplistic introduction to major religious beliefs, for younger children.

RH

Bangladesh

Michael Marsh
Franklin Watts, ISBN 0-7496-5379-5, £12.99 (hbk)

From the 'Country File' series, *Bangladesh* presents up-to-date information on the land and its people and examines the general physical, cultural and economic characteristics of this country. It uses attractive photographs, pictures, maps, graphs and tables of key facts to present information on rural and urban life as well as on religious practices and customs. The singularity of urban life in the capital city, Dhaka, is noted by explaining that nearly half of all journeys taken there are by bicycle. The text is clear and not over-complicated, and the book has useful retrieval devices such as a glossary, an index and a table of contents, as well as headings, diagrams and suggested websites to assist information searches by younger readers. The graphics and data range in difficulty, including, for example, quite detailed information on population density as well as simpler information on sport and leisure. This makes *Bangladesh* useful for older and younger children alike. The book is perfect for individual, group or class work on a particular theme, and encourages the study of issues such as flooding near the Ganges, the causes of such flooding and its effects on the people of low-lying countries such as Bangladesh. This approach might help readers to compare instances of flooding in developing and developed countries, or to examine and assess the causes and effects of floods and disasters in a more global context. (11+)

GO'C

Beliefs and Cultures: Muslim

Richard Tames
Franklin Watts, ISBN 0-7496-5232-2, £5.99 (pbk)

An introduction to Islam and to its followers, this guide from the 'Beliefs and Cultures' series gives a short biography of Muhammad and outlines his teachings and the central beliefs of Islamic faith. The origin and content of the Qur'an is covered, together with explanations of Muslim festivals and significant occasions,

including details about the fast of Ramadan. The functions and layout of mosques, as well as the significance and content of the pilgrimage to Mecca, are also explained. The role of Islam in general family life is shown through descriptions of Muslim customs and ceremonies marking birth, marriage and death. The book is clear, and plentifully illustrated with well-chosen photographs from all over the world, illustrating the spread and the cultural diversity of Islam. There is also a small number of suggested activities, intended to provide additional insight, but these seem a little uninspiring and underdeveloped, particularly considering the very fine tradition of arts and crafts in the Islamic world. However, this is an informative and well-illustrated book, providing a direct and immediate introduction to the Muslim faith and culture, and would be most successful when used with an interested adult's own suggestions to bring Islamic arts to life.

JFi

Bóthar an tSíoda: Taiscéalaíocht thar Tír

Paul Strathern, arna aistriú ag Seán Ó Cadhain
An Gúm, ISBN 1-85791-318-3, €8.25 (clúdach bog/pbk)

Fascinating for readers with excellent Irish and an interest in the ancient world. This is a book with great dip-in appeal, and it may attract even those not usually prepared to make the effort to read in Irish, though the exotic proper names are a bit difficult to cope with. A useful glossary and a helpful table of dates and events are included. Is aoibhinn an leabhar é seo, agus é maisithe go healaíonta, le griangrafanna daite den chuid is mó. Tugann sé cur síos ar stair Bhóthar an tSíoda (agus bealaí eile mar é) ón tSín go dtí an Eoraip, agus an scéal roinnte go caoithiúil i ngiotaí beaga soléite. Tugtar dhá leathanach ar aghaidh a chéile d'achan fo-ábhar; agus ar achan dá leathanach tá príomhthéacs, griangrafanna agus learáidí eile, agus sleachta beaga anseo is ansiúd leagtha amach i mboscaí. Déantar cur síos iontach suimiúil ar chultúir agus ar chreidimh an

Domhain Thoir. Ní hiad na páistí amháin a chuirfidh suim sa leabhar seo. (12+)

SP

Carrying

Gwenyth Swain
Milet, ISBN 1-84059-128-5 English/Urdu, £5.99 (pbk)

Carrying is a tiny dual-language picture book, from the 'Small World' series, that investigates what people around the world carry. It adopts a conversational tone and asks the young reader questions such as 'What do you carry?' and 'Does someone, sometimes carry you?' Twenty-three beautiful pictures of children and adults from different countries and cultural backgrounds are included. These photographs show images of play and everyday life: we see, for example, an Inuit girl carrying her doll, and boys in Thailand taking part in a water-carrying festival. Some background information is given on each picture; however, it would have been better had this included each person's name and the location of their home within the country mentioned. Nevertheless, *Carrying* offers a wealth of opportunities to prompt discussion about people and cultural traditions and has some useful tips for adults sharing the book with a child. It suggests that children might examine how ways of carrying things differ and are the same around the world, and that children might be asked to attempt to carry small items in ways similar to those featured. The other books in this series – *Smiling*, *Eating* and *Celebrating* – are all available in English with Arabic, Bengali, Chinese, Gujarati, Punjabi, Turkish or Vietnamese. (4+)

GO'C

Can't Lose Cant: a book of Cant, the old language of Irish Travellers

written by children in County Kildare, Ireland
Kids' Own Publishing Partnership, ISBN 1-902432-18-5, €20 (hbk)

This is the world's first book on Cant, the traditional language of the Irish Travelling community. Importantly, the book is designed as a primer, allowing the reader to learn the language cumulatively and methodically. Illustrated throughout with images (cut and pasted and slyly set on squared paper to suggest a textbook that is simultaneously an exercise book), it allows word and image to work together to produce a practical guide that silently evokes the historically fractured nature of the relationship between the Travelling community and its settled counterparts. This is a highly imaginative, accessible and passionately conceived celebration of diversity, enabling communication, mutual respect and exchange among diverse elements in Ireland. The fact that it is authored by children for children is enormously hopeful and promising. In a broader context, as the introduction suggests, it 'offers children the opportunity to become teachers to their peers', and presents a model 'for raising awareness of language diversity'.

AP

Geeta's Day: Dawn to Dusk in an Indian Village

Prodeepta Das
Frances Lincoln, ISBN 0-7112-2024-7, £5.99 (pbk)

Geeta's Day is an informative and visually appealing depiction of a typical day in the life of a young girl in an Indian village. Particularly notable is the village children's freedom to explore and play, unhindered by the controlling presence of supervising adults – a thing of the past for many children in today's world. The importance of the extended family and the local community in Indian culture is effectively evoked both in the text and in the stunning photographs, as is the way in which religious practice is seamlessly interwoven with everyday life. The vibrant colours of the people's clothing and the intense sunlight captured in the photographs create a celebratory tone. Hindi words are interspersed throughout the book and listed at the back in a useful glossary. An appendix contains information about India's history, geographical features and culture. This attractive book would be an invaluable resource in any primary school classroom.

CNíBh

Daisy Bates

Elisabeth Monkhouse and Emmett Arrigan, arna aistriú ag Ciardha Ní Mháirtín, arna mhaisiú ag Mary Arrigan
An Gúm, ISBN 1-85791-181-4, €6.29 (clúdach bog/pbk)

This is the story of a pioneering woman who lived an unconventional, adventurous life. A woman of culture and learning, she emigrated to Australia in her early twenties. After marrying twice in Australia and bearing a son, she worked as a reporter in London for five years. Returning to Australia, she devoted her remaining years to the aboriginal people, living with them and absorbing their culture. Her book *My Natives and I* was published in her old age. She died in 1951 in Adelaide.

Seo scéal eachtraíochta faoi bhean a chaith an chuid is mó dá saol i measc bundúchasaigh na hAstráile. I dTiobraid Árann a tógadh í, i lár an naoú haois déag. Chothaigh a sean-mháthair an dúil a bhí ag Daisy sa léann, sa mhiotaseolaíocht agus sa domhan mór. Phós sí dhá uair san Astráil agus saolaíodh mac di, ach bhí sí i gcónaí neamhspleách agus, tar éis roinnt blianta, thug sí aghaidh ar Londain agus d'oibrigh ann mar iriseoir. Nuair a thuig sí cruachás na mbundúchasach san Astráil d'fhill sí ar an tír sin agus chaith sí an chuid eile dá saol ina measc ag foghlaim uathu, agus ag troid a gcás. Agus í ina seanbhean foilsíodh a leabhar, *My Natives and I*. Fuair sí bás sa bhliain 1951 in Adelaide. (12+)

LÉARÁID Ó DAISY BATES

CQ

Goddesses: A World of Myth and Magic

Burleigh Mutén, illustrated by Rebecca Guay
Barefoot Books, ISBN 1-84148-076-6, £12.99 (hbk)

This is both an information source and an excellent reference guide to the great world goddesses. The entries are alphabetically presented, and a phonetic guide to each one's names and country of origin is included. Some basic information is given about each goddess. A quite extensive range of cultures is represented here, and the book is really impressive in terms of the sources used and the detailed information given on each entry. Though the information presented is very accessible and can be navigated through the index at the back of the book, the omission of a table of contents means that the young reader might have difficulty negotiating the book's contents. The book is quite lavishly illustrated, with classic-style panels and portraits of most of the goddesses.

FO'S

Here Comes Our Bride!

Ifeoma Onyefulu
Frances Lincoln, ISBN 1-84507-047-X, £10.99 (hbk)

This engaging wedding story is set in Benin City in Nigeria and narrated with admirable immediacy by a young boy, Ekinadose, with whom the child reader in middle to upper primary school will readily identify. Excitement mounts as Ekinadose impatiently watches preparations being made for his uncle's wedding. The traditional African ceremony is followed by a church wedding some months later. Both the solemnity of marriage and the joyous sense of celebration shared by the whole community are effectively conveyed through the child's eyes. The vibrant photographs provide a particularly illuminating insight into Nigerian custom and tradition, and additional information is provided in useful information boxes that are interspersed throughout the book without detracting from the flow of the narrative. One of the most striking photographs in the book depicts the happy couple in traditional wedding dress, its beautiful, warm, earthen hues contrasting effectively with the more Western church wedding depicted in the following photograph – a testament to the happy co-existence of both traditions.

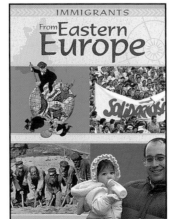

CNiBh

Hot Jazz Special

Jonny Hannah
Walker Books, ISBN 0-7445-92038, £12.99 (hbk)

Moody blues permeate the pages of this stunning presentation of a night at the Body and Soul Café – and what a night, as Jelly Roll Morton, Billie Holliday, Gene Krupa, Duke Ellington and many other greats of jazz all appear to blow the blues away in spectacular style. Each spread is devoted to an artist, capturing the period and the essence of the music. Hannah's handmade poster-style art encapsulates the ambience of a jazz club; all you need is an old-style record player and a stack of 78s as you turn the pages. But CDs will do! Great for those who already love jazz, and for anyone who you think should. (8+)

VC

Immigrants From Eastern Europe

Sarah Horrell
Franklin Watts, ISBN 0-7496-4534-2, £6.99 (pbk)

This informative and compact book examines the history of migration from eastern Europe to the West, its causes, and the subsequent impact of this migration on the lives of immigrants and on their new host countries. A map identifies present-day eastern Europe, while photographs and pictures help to inform the reader about the different ethnic groups of this area. The book deals mainly with immigrants to North America and Britain in the mid-twentieth century, and particular attention is paid to Jewish migration. Improvements in world travel, the pull of greater employment opportunities and the push of religious and political persecution are outlined as factors in the large-scale migration of the twentieth century. The vulnerability of many early immigrants to unscrupulous employers, and the hardship and isolation they often endured, are reminders of the problems commonly faced by immigrants nowadays. This book helps to explain some recent conflicts. It notes, for example, how growing tensions occurred between ethnic groups in eastern Europe, and the hostilities that developed between Jewish immigrants and the Arab population in Palestine. Interesting pictorial evidence, helpful captions and information points, timelines and the clarity of its overall design make this an attractive information book for readers in second-level schools.

GO'C

Jesus and Christianity

Alan Brown
Hodder Wayland, ISBN 0-7502-3703-1, £6.99 (pbk)

This book, from the 'Great Religious Leaders' series, details what is known of Jesus's life, teachings and influence over two thousand years. Jesus lived a very simple life with his parents until he was thirty, and spent his last three years teaching the word of God before being tried and executed. He challenged people's way of thinking, encouraging them to love their enemies, asking them not to judge other people harshly and to forgive wrongdoing in others. He was concerned for the poor and the outcasts of society. Today, there are two billion Christians in the world. A good mixture of text and pictures presents clearly the key elements of the religion, and information is included on the main festivals, rites of passage, sacred texts and branches of Christianity. Other books in the series include *Moses and Judaism*, *Guru Nanak and Sikhism*, *Krishna and Hinduism*, *Muhammad and Islam* and *Buddha and Buddhism*.

AMK

Masks and Performance with Everyday Materials

Gita Wolf, illustrated by Anushka Ravishanker
Tara Publishing, ISBN 81-86211-47-0, £10.99 (hbk)

This is a book that speaks directly to the reader, adult or child, though the authors do stress that it is best suited to readers over twelve. The direct address to the reader gives the book a clear edge over more run-of-the-mill craft books on the market. The book is based on the authors' experience of working with a group of students to create masks and stage performances based on four different traditions in Southern India. The masks were made from everyday materials and the performance created by the students themselves. This is neither simply a craft book nor a book about performance, but a delightful account of how these teachers worked with students, mask-makers and director to create a piece of art that celebrates a culture. The book itself is beautifully made, with colour photographs stuck onto brown cardboard pages. Well worth investing in!

FO'S

Our Culture: Jewish

Jenny Wood
Franklin Watts, ISBN 0-7496-5043-5, £5.99 (pbk)

Books about different faiths are valuable resources for schools, libraries and homes, in that they can promote a greater understanding of, and respect for, different religious practices and traditions. In *Our Culture: Jewish*, the importance of Jewish family life and religious rituals is conveyed through the use of photographs, largely of one particular family. The book gives some interesting, though basic, information about home life, the celebration of festivals, kosher food and the synagogue. A particular focus is given to festivals such as the Sukkot or harvest festival. While a book for younger readers cannot be over-complex, some further information and explanations, had they been included, would have given greater insight into the Jewish faith. For example, while the customs observed during Passover are noted, no explanation is given about what this festival commemorates. It would also have been interesting to explain that the hat worn in some of the photographs, a *kippah*, is worn as a mark of respect to God. While the book deals with minor festivals such as Hanukkah and Purim, no mention is made of the major festival of Yom Kippur. A simple glossary explains words from the text, but no guide to their pronunciation is given. Non-Jewish readers will need to seek out further information to explain more fully the Jewish religion and its associated customs and traditions. Nevertheless, this book is useful as an introduction to the Orthodox Jewish faith, particularly for younger readers. (7+)

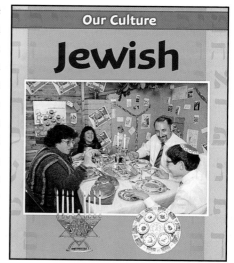

GO'C

Puppets around the World

Meryl Doney
Franklin Watts, ISBN 0-7496-4548-2, £5.99 (pbk)

This informative book from the 'Discover Other Cultures' series features puppets from Poland, India, China, Britain, Mali, Tunisia, Indonesia, Greece, Turkey, Japan and Burma. Beginning with a short history of puppets, and listing items useful when compiling a puppet-making kit, the book describes and illustrates puppets, explaining how each is used in the theatre of its country. Details about wooden, hand, shadow, string and many other puppets provide an effective introduction to other cultures; descriptions of the puppets' uses in storytelling and theatrical traditions are especially interesting. The book contains useful addresses, a glossary and step-by-step guides showing how to make all the puppets, along with advice on how to make stages and put on plays. Nearly everything is relatively easy to make, and would be most useful in senior primary classes, the materials being, for the most part, readily available. The book is copiously illustrated with photographs, diagrams and maps, and there are plenty of puppets to choose from, from the simple to the more elaborate. All provide a wonderful, and unusual, introduction to the cultures of other countries, as well as the opportunity to actively engage in further storytelling when the newly created puppets are ready for their debut.

JFi

Saying Goodbye: A Special Farewell to Mama Nkwelle

Ifeoma Onyefulu
Frances Lincoln, ISBN 0-7112-1701-7, £5.99 (pbk)

The death of a loved one is treated with warmth and sensitivity in this beautiful picture book, in which a young boy describes the funeral of his great-grandmother in Nkwelle village in eastern Nigeria. The predominant tone is one of celebration and togetherness, as is immediately apparent from the cheerful cover design and the colourful photographs throughout. All of Mama Nkwelle's relations take part in the preparations for the ceremony, and the whole community gathers to pay tribute to her through prayer, song, dance and storytelling. The final photographic sequence, in which the young boy plants palm kernels given to him by his great-grandmother, is poignantly symbolic of the continuing cycle of life and its potential richness. While depicting in some detail the funeral customs and rites of a particular culture, Onyefulu strikes a universal chord in this heart-warming affirmation of life and of love. (6+)

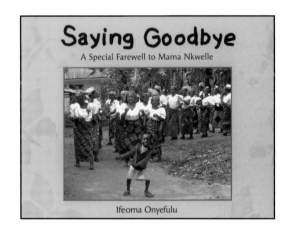

CNiBh

The Changing Face of Ireland

Kay Barnham, photographs by Chris Fairclough
Hodder Wayland, ISBN 0-7502-4072-5, £11.99 (hbk)

This is a large-format fact book about contemporary Ireland, with the emphasis on change. The chapters detail how both the Irish environment and the Irish people are changing under the impact of rapid development. The selection of photos is well chosen, conveying a picture of a lively and multicultural society. Photo and text inserts of real people enliven the overly statistical approach to conveying changes. The heavy burden of statistics does make the text rather turgid, and it reads more like a set of notes than a coherent introduction to contemporary Irish society. On the positive side, there are none of the usual clichés, and the only reference to bogs is to the conflict between depletion and environmental conservation. In my view, the brief history section does contain errors – the section on the War of Independence, partition and Civil War, for example, is hopelessly wrong: the Civil War was about the authenticity of the sovereignty offered in the Treaty, and partition had little or nothing to do with it. Countries covered in this series include Malaysia, Mexico, Nigeria, Peru, Poland, Russia, South Africa, Spain, Sweden, Thailand, the Caribbean and the Czech Republic.

MM

The Life of Stephen Lawrence

Verna Allette Wilkins, illustrated by Lynne Willey
Tamarind Press, ISBN 1-870516-58-3, £10.99 (hbk)

On 22 April 1993, Stephen Lawrence was murdered while waiting for a bus. His killers have not yet been brought to justice. This book is a brave and interesting attempt to document the life of a young man who was killed for no reason other than the colour of his skin. Wilkins appears to have carried out a series of interviews in writing the book, and she highlights the normality of Stephen's life throughout. Siblings, teachers and parents provide anecdotes about Stephen that the author has assimilated and rewritten, in a somewhat patronising tone, for the young reader. While they emphasise the brutal nature of the attack and the tragic effects on Stephen's family, the narrative of these personal stories does not always sustain interest. The book is often interrupted by references to the vicious nature of the murder that jar with the sentimental tone of the majority of the text. While this is an important attempt to preserve the memory of Stephen Lawrence and call for justice as well as racial tolerance, the patronising style of writing and the unimaginative illustrations detract from the magnitude and significance of the subject matter. (10–12)

PW

The Story of Divaali

retold by Jatinder Verma, illustrated by Nilesh Mistry
Barefoot Books, ISBN 1-902283-98-8, £5.99 (pbk)

This is the very complex story of how Lord Vishnu, when told that the demon Ravana's breath has eclipsed the sun, comes to earth in the form of handsome Rama. When the high priest insists that he take a wife, he goes to Mithila, where he sees and falls in love with Princess Sita, whose hand in marriage is also desired by Ravana. Love wins out and Rama brings Sita back to his kingdom, only to be exiled by his stepbrother. Rama, Sita and Rama's young brother Lakshmama spend fourteen years in the forest. Ravana kidnaps Sita, taking her to his kingdom. Rama and Lakshmama rescue her with the help of Hanuman, God of the Wind. When they return to their kingdom, all the people celebrate and the celebration becomes the Festival of Light, Divaali. The story is a complex retelling that introduces the young reader in senior primary to many of the gods and demons of Hindu culture. It is quite simply told in direct narrative. The wonderful images by Nilesh Mistry are beautifully stylised, not just giving the story a sense of place but also retaining its mythological backdrop.

FO'S

Thura's Diary: A Young Girl's Life in War-Torn Baghdad

Thura Al-Windawi
Puffin Books, ISBN 0-141-31769-8, £5.99 (pbk)

Thura is a student, from an educated, fairly privileged, liberal Muslim background. This makes her more like her English-speaking readers – and harder to slot into a prejudiced view of the world – than many other young people who have experienced the war in Iraq. Her diary begins in March 2003, shortly before the American (and other countries') invasion of Iraq, and ends in June 2003, after the official ending of the war. There are one or two add-on pieces, bringing us up to the capture of Saddam Hussein in December 2003. Thura is no Anne Frank, and her diary, clearly written with publication in mind, is not an intimate account of her inner life and thoughts, though it does deal with the day-to-day life of Thura and her family. It's not a 'great read', and we do not feel particularly close to the people in it. But that's not what this book is about. Its value is as a piece of living documentary. It is likely to form a first step in the political education of many young people, giving them an insight into what life is like in wartime, and it would be most useful as a starting point for discussion on world affairs, human rights and the morality or immorality of war, especially this war.

PHOTOGRAPH FROM THURA'S DIARY

SP

When I Was A Soldier

Valerie Zenatti
Bloomsbury, ISBN 0-7475-7566-5, £5.99 (pbk)

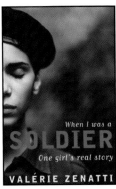

This fascinating and unusual book details the author's two-year period of mandatory service in the Israeli army, after leaving school at eighteen. Zenatti writes well, her observations are sharp and pithy, and she gives a remarkably objective assessment of the military environment in which she finds herself. Military combat is portrayed as an essential element of Israeli society, and is viewed by many as a panacea to the country's complex problems. Ordinary life is infused with all things military, to the extent that people appear virtually unaware of war's devastating consequences, incapable of imagining life without it. The teenagers in Israel's army are viewed as heroes by its citizens, and the author's strong, cynical personality mirrors accurately the temperament of the Israeli people themselves: 'sarcastic humour and contempt are a means of communication everyone understands.' For this reason, it is difficult to warm to the people of this warring country, but the book is an excellent and absorbing portrayal of one girl's experience of the propagandist training she is obliged to undergo. It makes one question the wider impact of military manipulation on so many impressionable young minds.

JMi

Where We Live

Valerie Guin
Franklin Watts, ISBN 0-7496-5437-6, £11.99 (hbk)

This information book, from the 'One World' series, explores homes around the world. It depicts a variety of house types and develops the concept that a home is a place that affords shelter and security. It groups homes into simple categories, such as wooden houses, houses on legs, and straw-roofed dwellings. The book is designed for young readers; it is highly visual and contains attractive colour photographs that show everyday domestic scenes. Words highlighted in the text are explained in a glossary. Other reference devices included are an index, a table of contents and an informative map showing all the countries mentioned. This book would help to develop children's awareness of the diversity of homes throughout the world, leading them to an understanding that the physical designs of homes, the building materials used and their location vary according to climate, economics and available local

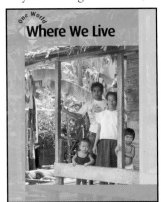

materials. Examples of homes from the developing world and the Western world are shown, and this highlights similarities and differences in both their forms and their functions. Recommended to promote an understanding of the rights of all peoples to shelter and homes. (8–10)

GO'C

Whiddin to the Gauras: Talking to our Own

written and compiled by Eleanor Gormally
Veritas, ISBN 1-85390-863-0, €4.95 (pbk)

This book emerged from a partnership between Mary Immaculate College of Education and the Limerick Travellers Development Group. It is an important and ground-breaking study. The researchers – Mags Casey, Ann O'Donoghue, Bridgie O'Donoghue and Ann O'Driscoll – are themselves members of the Travelling community; they undertook a preliminary training course to enable them to interview primary-school children in a professional way. Their pride in their achievement is clear. They evaluate their experience very frankly, outlining the challenges, what worked well, and how they might do things differently in the future. The study has the great advantage of avoiding the condescension that can so often be almost unavoidable in academic research, where interviewers often seem to come from positions of external power and author-ity. What emerges is a big and complex picture of the views of Traveller children, and a sense of what things are important in their lives. There is not much consolation for those of us who like to think and hope that school is a positive experience for Traveller children. It is clear that they feel they are in an alien world that has little relevance to their real lives, and they are wary. At the same time, a favourite teacher is often mentioned. In a series of strong and positive recommen-dations, this study calls on the world of education to make changes. Everyone interested in the study of minority cultures, disadvantage, education, and academic research in its relationship to wider communities should read this. Every school, primary and secondary, should have a copy.

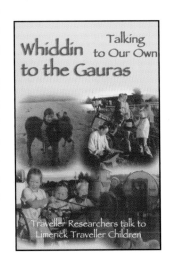

CK

Public Libraries: Responding to New Community Needs

Public libraries are expanding their stocks and services to meet the demands of Ireland's changing population. They have also been instrumental in promoting the inclusion of multicultural and dual-language books in school libraries.

IMPERCEPTIBLY, IN THE MID-1990s, Ireland became host to more and more emigrants and became, visibly and audibly, an increasingly multicultural society. For libraries, as for every other government agency, the changing composition of Irish society had varied implications. One of the major strengths of a public library is the diversity of needs that it serves. Balanced stock selection had always ensured that children's libraries had books on various countries for geography projects, books on world religions and, of course, fairy tales from around the world; and as most of the books came from English publishers there was always multi-ethnic representation in fiction and information. But, generally, books on other cultures and traditions were relatively rare.

As librarians became aware of the changing population, they began to source books that provided positive cultural affirmation. Librarians are always conscious of the power of language, illustration and photographs to provoke thought, heighten awareness and enrich cultural understanding. Books, especially in school or crèche situations, play a vital role in facilitating a blend of cultural integration, preservation and interchange.

The publication of *Changing Faces – Changing Places* (2001) gave librarians an invaluable resource from which to select a wide range of books for their children's libraries. In Dublin City Libraries, a copy of each title reviewed was bought for the twenty-two branches in the system. Demand is created through promotion, and on-going displays create awareness of the increasing range of material available. There is statistical evidence that books from *Changing Faces – Changing Places* are being borrowed regularly. For instance, over a three-year period, *My Granny Went to Market* (1998) has been issued two hundred and two times, Ifeoma Onyfulu's *Emeka's Gift* (1998) has been issued fifty-four times, and *The Coming of the Night: A Yoruba Creation Myth from West Africa* (2000) has been issued one hundred and fifty-one times.

A cultural awareness training day, which included discussion of the books available for children, was also organised for staff. In Dublin City Libraries' School Service, multiple copies of each title were purchased and displayed. When these were pointed out to teachers, the teachers were interested and selected books from the display. In subsequent years, teachers have begun to ask for specific titles, for books about countries from which their pupils come or for picture dictionaries. One school requested books in Swedish and Arabic so that the children in their school could read books written in their own languages; they felt that the languages of the children in their school should be represented in the school library. Childcare workers have begun to ask for multicultural books for the children and to inform themselves about cultural differences. The demand is growing, albeit very slowly, and perhaps mainly from those professionally involved in working with multi-ethnic groups.

In April 2004 the *Libraries and Cultural Diversity* research project, funded by the Department of the Environment, Heritage and Local Government and the library authorities, was initiated. The aim of the project is to 'explore how Irish libraries can provide a better service to the current multicultural society'. The preliminary research phase surveyed all public library authorities in Ireland and examined the library requirements of members of culturally diverse communities. One of the findings of the survey of city and county librarians was that over seventy percent of library authorities provided collections of materials in community languages, and dual-language materials, especially for children. One library authority incorporated dual-language stock into an exhibition, which toured primary schools. Another library authority encourages teachers to take multicultural books as a proportion of their annual allocation. The research project will produce a report, which will include recommendations for future library provision.

Certainly there are many challenges and great opportunities ahead. Each person, young or old, is enriched through positive new experiences; and libraries are ideally placed, in their communities and in the schools, to provide focal points for cultural interchange and celebration through books and events.

BOOKS DISCUSSED IN THIS ARTICLE:

Blackstone, Stella and Bernard Lodge, *My Granny Went to Market: A Round the World Counting Rhyme*. Barefoot Books, 1998, 1901223434

Coghlan, Susanna, Mary Fitzpatrick and Lucy O'Dea (eds), *Changing Faces – Changing Places: A Guide to Multicultural Books for Children*. IBBY Ireland, 2001, 0954135202

Onyefulu, Ifeoma, *Emeka's Gift*. Frances Lincoln, 1998, 0711212554

Riordan, James and Jenny Stow, *The Coming of the Night: A Yoruba Creation Myth from West Africa*. Frances Lincoln, 2000, 071121378X

RESOURCES

AND LISTINGS

ADDITIONAL RESOURCES

CLASSROOM AND LIBRARY RESOURCES

A Bridge of Children's Books
Jella Lepman
The remarkable autobiography of Jella Lepman who returned to Germany after the Second World War and founded the International Youth Library and IBBY
The O'Brien Press, 2002, hbk, 0-86278-783-1
www.obrien.ie

Guide to Development Education Resources 2004–2005
Contains details on over ninety titles aimed directly at the primary sector
Available from: Development Cooperation Ireland Resource Centre

Guidelines for Traveller Education in Primary School
Compiled by ESRU
Department of Education and Science, 0-7557-1171-8
www.education.ie

INTO Intercultural Guidelines for Schools/Treoirlínte Idirchultúrtha CMÉ do Scoileanna
www.into.ie

Intercultural Education in the Primary School
Guidelines designed to provide support for all the members of the school community. Includes teaching materials, exemplars for classroom activities to support the development of intercultural awareness and competence
National Council for Curriculum and Assessment, 2005, pbk
www.ncca.ie

Mantra Lingua produces a number of CD-Roms, audio CDs, wall charts and other classroom resources
www.mantralingua.com

Milly, Molly
Gill Pittar
A series of books that describe the adventures of two little girls and are written to promote the acceptance of diversity and the learning of life skills
www.millymolly.com

SOME STORIES WRITTEN WITH TRAVELLER CULTURE IN MIND

A Horse for Joe; Two for One
Wiltshire Traveller Education
Tel: +44 1225 771687   Fax: +44 1225 771681

Horses; Tom; Where's Mouse; After School; I Spy
Cardiff Traveller Education Service
info@traved.org   www.traved.org/publications.asp

Melissa to the Rescue
Avon Consortium Traveller Education Service
lynds-howells@southglos.gov.uk

Moving Pasts
Newham Traveller Education Service
anthea.wormington@newham.gov.uk

My Little Box of Books; Where's My Teddy
Durham & Darlington Education Service for Travelling People
Tel: +44 1740 656998   Fax: +44 1740 657792

Ruby's Rabbit; Sean's Wellies
Norfolk Traveller Education Service
frances.sinclair.edu@norfolk.gov.uk

Tess the Traveller
Friends, Families and Travellers
fft@communitybase.org   www.gypsy-traveller.org

Two Little Travellers
The Advisory Service for the Education of Travellers
traaved@a-s-et.demon.co.uk   www.a-s-e-t.demon.co.uk

Wally's First Boxing Match
Sutton and Merton Traveller Education
kate.evans@sutton.gov.uk

SOURCES FOR RESOURCES

Amnesty International Shops
Seán Mac Bride House, Fleet Street, Dublin 2. Tel: +353 1 6776361
Amnesty International Shop, Middle Street, Galway.
info@amnesty.ie   www.amnesty.ie

Children's Books Ireland Library
17 North Great Georges Street, Dublin 1. Tel: +353 1 8727475
info@childrensbooksireland.com   www.childrensbooksireland.com

Christian Aid
www.christianaid.org.uk/learn/schools

Development Cooperation Ireland Resource Centre
Development Studies Centre, Kimmage Manor, Whitehall Road, Dublin 12. Tel: +353 1 4064386/380
info@dsckim.ie

National Youth Council of Ireland
www.youth.ie/deved

Trócaire Resource Centres
12 Cathedral Street, Dublin 1. Tel: +353 1 8743875
info@cs.trocaire.org
9 Cook Street, Cork. Tel: +353 21 4275622   sheila@ck.trocaire.org
50 King Street, Belfast BT1 6AD. Tel: 048 90 238586
info@bl.trocaire.org   www.trocaire.org

UNICEF – United Nations Children's Fund
www.unicef.org

Young people's website: www.unicef.org/voy

Veritas
7–8 Lower Abbey Street, Dublin 1. Tel: +353 1 8788177
sales@veritas.ie   www.veritas.ie

USEFUL PUBLICATIONS

All of the following contain reviews of, and/or articles about, multicultural children's books.

PERIODICALS

Bookbird: A Journal of International Children's Literature
A refereed journal published quarterly by IBBY. Contains articles about books and reading from a wide variety of cultures and countries.
Edited by Valerie Coghlan and Siobhán Parkinson
ISSN: 0006 7377
Subscriptions to: journals@utoronto.ca   www.ibby.org

Books for Keeps
Features articles, book reviews and interviews with authors and illustrators. Six per annum
Edited by Rosemary Stones
Subscriptions to: booksforkeeps@btinternet.com
www.booksforkeeps.co.uk

Inis: The Magazine of Children's Books Ireland
Contains reviews and articles on Irish and international children's books. Four per annum
Edited by Patricia O'Doherty
Free to members of Children's Books Ireland (CBI) or €4 from some bookshops.
Subscriptions to: info@childrensbooksireland.com
www.childrensbooksireland.com

Metro Éireann
Multicultural newspaper. Publishes some book reviews.
www.metroeireann.com

The School Librarian
Journal of the School Library Association. Contains articles on children's literature and school library organisation and reviews of recent books, CD-ROMs and websites across the age ranges. Four per annum
Edited by Ray Lonsdale and Chris Brown
Free to members of SLARI and SLANI
Subscriptions to: info@SLA.org.uk   www.sla.org.uk

Reading News
Newsletter of the Reading Association of Ireland. Links with International Reading Association publications and discusses literacy issues in Ireland.
Membership: webmaster@reading.ie   www.reading.ie

BOOKS AND BROCHURES

BookFest
The annual recommended reading guide produced for the Children's Book Festival. It includes reviews and recommendations of over two hundred titles.
Free from CBI, bookshops and libraries

Changing Faces – Changing Places: A Guide to Multicultural Books in Ireland
Reviews of over a hundred and fifty multicultural books for children, with articles.
IBBY Ireland, 2001, 0954135202
info@irelandliterature.com   www.ibbyireland.ie

Children Between Worlds: Intercultural Relations in Books for Children and Young Adults
Fifty books about tolerance and open-mindedness towards other people. Internationale Jugendbibliothek (International Youth Library), 2002

Hello, Dear Enemy! Picture Books for Peace and Tolerance
A selection of one hundred titles. Internationale Jugendbibliothek, 2002

The White Ravens 2004: An Annual Selection of International Children's and Youth Literature
Issues from previous years are also available. Internationale Jugendbibliothek, 2004
information@ijb.de   www.ijb.de

IBBY Honour List 2004
A biennial selection of recently published titles, from over sixty countries, that are nominated by the national sections of IBBY for their outstanding writing, illustrations or translation.
ibby@ibby.org   www.ibby.org

WEBSITES FOR BOOK REVIEWS

Achuka: www.achuka.com

Book Trust (young people's section): www.booktrusted.co.uk

Carol-Hurst's children's literature site: www.carolhurst.com

Children's Books Ireland: www.childrensbooksireland.com

Cool Reads: www.coolreads.com

My Home Library: www.myhomelibrary.org

Rollercoaster: www.rollercoaster.ie

School-Library.Org: www.school-library.org

Reading Association of Ireland: www.reading.ie

USEFUL ORGANISATIONS

IRELAND

African Cultural Project
Tel: +353 1 878 0613   acp@indigo.ie

Amnesty International Irish Section
"Voice Our Concern" project.
Amnesty's human rights education initiative bringing together
transition year students and some of Ireland's best known writers.
Tel: +353 1 6776361   info@amnesty.ie   www.amnesty.ie

Bord na Leabhar Gaeilge
Guthán: +353 46 9430419   blg@leabhar.ie   www.leabhar.ie

Children's Books Ireland
Tel: +353 1 8727475   info@childrensbooksireland.com
www.childrensbooksireland.com

Children's and Schools Section, Dublin Public Libraries
www.dublincity.ie/livinginthecity/libraries/library services.asp
Tel +353 1 6744885

Concern
Republic of Ireland Tel: +353 1 417 7700
Northern Ireland Tel: 028 9033 1100
www.concern.net

Cultural Links
Tel: +353 25 37940   culturallinks@eircom.net

Development Education through Literature Programme
Writers in Schools, Poetry Ireland.
Tel: +353 1 4758601   writersinschools@poetryireland.ie
www.poetryireland.ie

The DICE Project
Tel: +353 1 497 0033   dice@cice.ie   www.cice.ie/dice

Foras na Gaeilge
Guthán: 1850 25 325 (ROI); 028 9089 0970 (NI)
eolas@forasnagaeilge.ie   www.forasnagaeilge.ie

IBBY Ireland
Tel: +353 1 678 8961   info@irelandliterature.com
www.ibbyireland.ie

Ireland Literature Exchange
Tel: +353 1 678 8961   info@irelandliterature.com
www.irelandliterature.com

Irish-Chinese Arts, Cultural and Shaolin Academy
kenmccue@dublinchinatown.com

Irish Society for the Study of Children's Literature
Celia.Keenan@spd.dcu.ie

Oxfam Ireland
Tel: +353 1 672 7662 (ROI); 028 9023 0220 (NI)
communications@oxfam.ie   www.oxfamireland.org

Pavee Point
Tel: +353 1 8780255   pavee@iol.ie   www.paveepoint.ie

Reading Association of Ireland
webmaster@reading.ie   www.readng.ie

Refugee Information Services
For information on cultural organisations and refugee services in
Ireland.
www.ris.ie

School Library Association, Republic of Ireland (SLARI)
slari@ireland.com
School Library Association of Northern Ireland (SLANI)
Tel: 028 91861199
www.sla.org.uk for both SLARI and SLANI

Trócaire
Tel: +353 1 6293333   info@trocaire.ie   www.trocaire.org

Waterford One World Centre
Tel: +353 51 873064   info@waterfordoneworldcentre.com
www.waterfordoneworldcentre.com

INTERNATIONAL

The Akha Book Project
The Akha Heritage Foundation
akha@akha.org   www.akha.org

Book Aid International
info@bookaid.org   www.bookaid.org

Booktrusted
www.booktrusted.co.uk

Brett Dillingham
brett@brettdillingham.com   www.brettdillingham.com

International Board on Books for Young People
ibby@ibby.org   www.ibby.org

Internationale Jugendbibliothek
International Youth Library
information@ijb.de   www.ijb.de

La Joie Par Les Livres
www.lajoieparleslivres.com French language only

LesArt
www.lesart.org German language only

Room to Read
info@roomtoread.org   www.roomtoread.org

PUBLISHERS

Andersen Press
Tel: +44 20 7840 8701   Fax: +44 20 7233 6263
andersenpress@randomhouse.co.uk   www.andersenpress.co.uk

An Gúm
Guthán: +353 1 8734700   Facs: +353 1 8731104
eolas@forasnagaeilge.ie

Barefoot Books
Tel: +44 1225 322400
info@barefootbooks.co.uk   www.barefootbooks.com

Barrington Stoke
Tel: +44 131 557 2020   Fax: +44 131 557 6060
info@barringtonstoke.co.uk   www.barringtonstoke.co.uk

Bloomsbury Children's Books
Tel: +44 20 7494 2111   Fax: +44 20 7434 0151
customerservices@bloomsbury.com   www.bloomsbury.com

Chicken House, The
Tel: +44 1373 454488   Fax: +44 1373 454499
chickenhouse@doublecluck.com   www.doublecluck.com

Cló Iar-Chonnachta
Guthán: +353 91 593307; +353 91 593362
cic@iol.ie   www.cic.ie

Cló Uí Bhriain
Guthán: +353 1 4923333   Facs: +353 1 4922777
sales@obrien.ie   www.obrien.ie

Egmont Children's Books
Tel: +44 20 7761 3500   Fax: +44 20 7761 3510
info@egmont.co.uk   www.egmont.co.uk

Frances Lincoln Children's Books
Tel: +44 20 7284 4009   Fax: +44 20 7845 0490
reception@franceslincoln.com www.franceslincoln.com

Franklin Watts
Tel: +44 20 7739 2929   Fax: +44 20 7739 2181
www.wattspub.co.uk
Imprints: Orchard Books

HarperCollins Children's Books
Tel: +44 20 8741 7070   Fax: +44 20 8307 4440
www.harpercollinschildrensbooks.co.uk
Imprints: Collins

Hodder Children's Books
Tel: +44 20 7873 6000   Fax: +44 20 7873 6024
www.hodderheadline.co.uk
Imprints: Hodder Wayland

Kid's Own Publishing Partnership
Tel: +353 71 9146364   Fax: +353 71 9146365
www.kidsown.ie

Little Tiger Press
Tel: +44 20 7385 6333   Fax: +44 20 7385 7333
info@littletiger.co.uk   www.littletigerpress.com

Mantra Lingua
Tel: +44 208 4455123   Fax: +44 208 4467745
info@mantralingua.com   www.mantralingua.com

Macmillan Children's Books
Tel: +44 20 7014 6000   Fax: +44 20 7014 6001
www.panmacmillan.com
Imprints: Young Picador

Mentor Press
Tel. +353 1 2952112   Fax: +353 1 2952114
info@mentor.ie

Milet
Tel: +44 20 7603 5477   Fax: +44 20 7610 5475
info@milet.com   www.milet.com

Móinín
Guthán: +353 65 7077256
moinin@eircom.net   www.moinin.ie

O'Brien Press, The
Tel: +353 1 4923333   Fax: +353 1 4922777
sales@obrien.ie   www.obrien.ie

Orion Children's Books
Tel: +44 20 7240 3444   Fax: +44 20 7379 6158
info@orionbooks.co.uk   www.orionbooks.co.uk
Imprints: Dolphin Paperbacks

Oxford University Press
Tel: +44 1865 556767   Fax: +44 1865 267912
webenquiry.uk@oup.com   www.oup.co.uk

Puffin Books
Tel: +44 20 7010 3000   Fax: +44 20 7010 6060
www.penguin.co.uk

Random House Children's Books
Tel: +44 20 8231 6800   Fax: +44 20 8231 6767
enquiries@randomhouse.co.uk   www.kidsatrandomhouse.co.uk
Imprints: Corgi, Doubleday, Red Fox, David Fickling Books

Simon & Schuster Children's Books
Tel: +44 20 7316 1900   Fax: +44 20 7316 0331/2
enquiries@simonandschuster.co.uk   www.simonsays.co.uk

Tamarind Books
Tel: +44 20 8866 8808
info@tamarindbooks.com

Tara Publishing
mail@tarabooks.com   www.tarabooks.com
Distributed in Ireland and the UK by Turnaround

Templar
Tel: +44 1306 876361   Fax: +44 1306 889097
info@templarco.co.uk www.templarco.co.uk

Usborne
Tel: +44 20 7430 2800   Fax: +44 20 7430 1562
mail@usborne.co.uk   www.usborne.com

Veritas Publications
Tel: +353 1 8788177   Fax: +353 1 8786507
sales@veritas.ie   www.veritas.ie

Walker Books
Tel: +44 20 7793 0909   Fax: +44 20 7587 1123
www.walkerbooks.co.uk

Áisínteacht Dáiliúchán Leabhar (ÁIS)
Distributor of Irish language books
Guthán: 01 616522   Facs: 01 616564

African Books Collective
Tel: 0044 1865 726686   Fax: 0044 1865 709265
orders@africanbookscollective.com
www.africanbookscollective.com

Letterbox Library
Tel: 0044 207 5034801   Fax: 0044 207 5034800
info@letterboxlibrary.com   www.letterboxlibrary.com

Turnaround
Tel: 0044 20 8829 3000   Fax: 020 8881 5088
enquiries@turnaround-uk.com   www.turnaround-psl.com

CONTRIBUTORS

Irene Barber is a primary school teacher in Dublin and was a school principal for many years. She is a regular reviewer of children's books and has contributed articles to a number of publications including *The Big Guide to Irish Children's Books*, Volumes 1 and 2.

Nathalie Beau is director of the National Children's Book Centre, Paris, and was founder and President of the French National Children's Bookseller Association. For the past number of years, she has been active in IBBY France.

Socorro Cano is founder member and principal of the Nicaraguan Environmental School, a primary school piloting an environmental education curriculum, situated in an area of extreme poverty in Managua, Nicaragua.

Helen Carr was managing editor of Veritas Publications. She has been a co-editor of *BookFest* for many years, and regularly reviews for *The Sunday Independent* and for *Inis*, the magazine of Children's Books Ireland. She currently works for The O'Brien Press.

Séamus Cashman is a poet and former publisher and founder of Wolfhound Press. He is the editor of the award-winning poetry anthology *Something Beginning With P*. Séamus currently works as a book consultant and is very involved with the Development Education through Literature Project administered by Poetry Ireland.

Alan Clarke is a professional illustrator whose work has been published by companies around the world. He is one of three artists who contributed to the award-winning *Something Beginning With P: New Poems from Irish Poets* published by The O'Brien Press.

Susanna Coghlan currently works in Cambodia. She was joint editor with Lucy O'Dea and Mary Fitzpatrick on *Changing Faces – Changing Places: A Guide to Multicultural Books for Children* published by IBBY Ireland in 2001.

Valerie Coghlan is librarian at the Church of Ireland College of Education, Dublin. She teaches courses on children's literature, including a module for the MA in Children's Literature at St Patrick's College, Dublin City University. She is co-editor of IBBY's international journal, *Bookbird*, and is vice-president of IBBY Ireland.

Clodagh Corcoran, a former specialist children's bookseller, established the Mother Goose Award for illustration in1979. She has served on the Yorkshire Arts Literature Panel and on the Federation of Children's Book Groups in the UK. Clodagh is a co-founder of the Irish Children's Book Trust. She has published two non-fiction books for adults and has edited several anthologoies for children. She currently reviews for *Books Ireland* and *Inis* magazine.

Gearóid Cronin worked as an editor with The O'Brien Press until recently. He formerly worked as a bilingual dictionary editor in Paris and in Edinburgh. He is a member of the Irish Translators' Association.

Brendan Culligan lectures in English Curriculum Studies in Froebel College of Education, Blackrock, County Dublin and is a long-serving member on the Board of the Reading Association of Ireland.

Judy Deacon is teaching principal in St Edan's NS, Ferns, County Wexford. She regularly reviews for *BookFest*, the reading list of Children's Book Festival.

Brett Dillingham coordinates the Alaska Reading Tutor Training programme and the Alaska Reading Institutes. He is a professional storyteller, and performs and teaches storytelling in Alaska, Canada, England, Ireland, Africa and the United States. He is the past president of the Alaska State Literacy Association (Alaska IRA), and a published poet and playwright.

Joanna Finegan studied Visual Communications at the National College of Art & Design and Library and Information Studies at University College Dublin. She is curator of the Department of Prints and Drawings at the National Library of Ireland.

Aubrey Flegg is an award-winning children's author. Formerly a geologist, Aubrey's earlier books draw on his experiences working in Ireland and Africa. *Wings Over Delft*, the first book in his *Louise* trilogy, won the Bisto Book of the Year award in 2004.

Jennifer Flegg has had a lifelong interest in children's literature. Born and educated in Dublin, she taught in France and worked in a library in Leicester before returning to teach in Dublin. She is now retired.

Susan Gallwey is the Development Education Officer at the Waterford One World Centre. The Centre works in partnership with the local community to educate and empower people to take action on global issues of social justice and human dignity. She designed and wrote the *Storyworlds* project with Beni Oburu.

Peter Heaney is a founding member of NINE [Northern Ireland Network Education]. He has initiated many projects including a project linking schools in Northern Ireland with schools in South Africa.

Rosemary Hetherington is a librarian in the Children's and Schools Section, Dublin City Council Libraries. She selects books for the primary school libraries in Dublin City.

Lucinda Jacob writes and illustrates children's books and poems. She leads workshops for children, reviews children's books and she also works with textiles. A number of her poems are included in anthologies for children published by Oxford University Press, Macmillan, and Hodder Children's Books.

Celia Keenan is a lecturer in English, and director of the MA programme in children's literature, at St Patrick's College, Dublin City University. She is a founder member and current president of the Irish Society for the Study of Children's Literature (ISSCL). She has co-edited *The Big Guide 2: Irish Children's Books* (2000) with Valerie Coghlan, and *Studies in Children's Literature: 1500–2000* (2004) with Mary Shine Thompson.

Anne-Marie Kelly is the Senior Librarian in the Children's and Schools Section, Dublin City Council Libraries. She coordinates library services for children and young adults in Dublin City.

Natasha Mac a'Bháird works for The O'Brien Press and regularly reviews books for children and adults. She is the author of *The Irish Bride's Survival Guide*.

Martin Maguire lectures in Irish history at Dundalk Institute of Technology. His research interests are the cultural history of religion, labour and working class history, and the history of state-formation. His work has been published in several historical journals and publications of collected essays. Martin reviews for *Inis*.

Nóra Maguire is a final year student of English and German in Trinity College Dublin, majoring in German Literature. She is a regular reviewer for *Inis*.

Jean Mason taught for six years in Singapore, Kuwait and Korea and for a further ten years in a school designated as disadvantaged. She now teaches in an Educate Together school in west Dublin.

Ken McCue is Director of Education for the Irish-Chinese Cultural Academy and a founding director of Sport Against Racism in Ireland. He is currently completing a post-graduate course in European Cultural Planning.

Matthew McDaniel is a committed activist who has lived and worked with the traditional Akha community for fourteen years. He currently works at UN level for Human Rights for the Akha people.

Teresa McGann completed a M Ed on the topic of Diversity in Education. She has worked as a primary school teacher in an area designated as disadvantaged since 1980. Teresa is now working with the Department of Education and Science as a Visiting Teacher for Travellers.

Jane Mitchell is an author of children's books and young adult fiction. Her first book won the Bisto Book of the Year award and her novels tackle difficult and challenging issues. Her latest works critically explore the long-term effects of war on children and the world that permits it. Jane works as a Project Manager in a national centre for people with physical disabilities.

Liz Morris worked as a Language Support teacher in an inner city Dublin school and currently teaches in an Educate Together school in west Dublin.

Lindsay Myers lectures in Italian at the National University of Ireland, Galway. Her research interests include Italian children's literature, literature and national identity and translation studies. She is a regular reviewer for *Inis*, and a member of both the ISSCL and the IRSCL.

Ciara Ní Bhroin lectures in English in Marino College of Education. She holds an MA and an MS Ed., specialising in the teaching of reading and writing. Recently published work includes articles on the adventure stories of Eilís Dillon, the fiction of Elizabeth O'Hara and the young adult novels of Robert Cormier. She is a regular reviewer of children's books for *Inis*.

Ursula Ní Dhálaigh was Senior Editor and later Publishing Director with The Educational Company and has done freelance work for Cois Life, The O'Brien Press, and the Department of Education and Science among others. She was for many years Chairperson of Bord na Leabhar Gaeilge, and a Board member of Ireland Literature Exchange which promotes inward and outward translation.

Máire Ní Dhonnchadha is a translator and interpreter. She currently works with Ireland Literature Exchange, an agency that promotes the literature of Ireland abroad. She is secretary of IBBY Ireland.

Colette Nic Aodha is a bi-lingual poet, short story writer and second-level teacher.

Áine Nic Gabhann completed her MA in Children's Literature in 2003. She teaches English in Coláiste Íosagáin. She is currently a judge on the Children's Books Ireland/Bisto awards panel and reviews for *Inis* magazine.

Beni Oburu is the founder of Cultural Links, an organisation which runs intercultural workshops in primary and second-level schools and also works with teachers through the colleges of education and in-service courses. She designed and wrote the Storyworlds project with Susan Gallwey. Beni is from Kenya and has been living in Ireland for eleven years.

Geraldine O'Connor lectures in social, environmental and scientific education at a College of Education, Dublin and is a member of the board of IBBY Ireland.

Annie O'Doherty, Dip. ECCE, is co-author of a training manual on the anti-bias approach in early education *Ar an mBealach*.

Patricia O'Doherty is a freelance writer and editor. Patricia is currently editor of *Inis*, the magazine of Children's Books Ireland.

Molly O'Duffy is a former primary school teacher and currently the Education Co-ordinator of the Dublin Inner City Partnership. She worked as support to the teaching staff of the Nicaragua Environmental School for three years.

Jane O'Hanlon is the Education Officer with Poetry Ireland and director of the Development Education through Literature Programme.

Larry O'Loughlin is the author of thirteen books, including poetry and fiction books; two of his books for young adults were listed in the *White Ravens* catalogue compiled by the International Youth Library. He is co-ordinator of the Development Education through Literature Programme administered by Poetry Ireland.

Finian O'Shea is lecturer in Education at the Church of Ireland College of Education in Dublin. He has served as a member of the executive of Reading Association of Ireland for many years and is currently chairing the RAI Book Award committee. He is a frequent reviewer for *Inis* magazine and a passionate advocate of quality literature for children.

Barbara O'Toole is the co-ordinator for the DICE Project (Development & Intercultural Education). She has worked in education since 1980 – as a primary teacher, as a teacher for children with emotional and behavioural difficulties in inner London, and as Head of Islington's Behaviour Management Team, supporting secondary schools in the borough to reduce exclusions.

Liz Page is the Administrative Director of the International Board on Books for Young People (IBBY). She was a founding member of JuKiBu, the Intercultural Children's Library in Basel, Switzerland. Later she was elected President of the Intercultural Children's Libraries Association of Switzerland. She has worked with IBBY since 1997.

Siobhán Parkinson is joint editor with Valerie Coghlan of *Bookbird*, the journal of IBBY. She is an award-winning writer of fiction for children, and also writes for adults. She is an active member of the Poetry Ireland Writers-in-Schools scheme. She teaches fiction writing at the Adult Education Centre, UCD, and is writer-in-residence at Marino College of Education.

A J Piesse is a Fellow of Trinity College Dublin and a Senior Lecturer in English Literature there. Her special interests include early Tudor education and representations of old age in children's books. She has published on these and other related areas in *Studies in Children's Literature 1500–2000* and in *Inis*.

Charlie Quinn works as a librarian in Fingal County Libraries and has reviewed Irish language and teen fiction for *BookFest* for many years.

Daragh Reddin is the Assistant Editor for Veritas Publications and has also contributed reviews to *BookFest*, the reading list of Children's Book Festival.

Carole Redford teaches English at St Patrick's College, Dublin. She reviews widely and has contributed chapters to a number of books on children's literature, most recently to *Studies in Children's Literature: 1500–2000* (2004).

Sarah Webb has been co-editor of *BookFest*, the annual recommended readling list of Children's Book Festival, for many years. She has worked as a children's buyer and marketing manager in the book trade and is now a best-selling author and a children's book consultant.

Pádraic Whyte is a PhD student, researching literature and film for children in Ireland. He is a Government of Ireland Research Scholar and studies in both the School of English and the School of Drama in Trinity College. Pádraic is the current secretary of the Irish Society for the Study of Children's Literature.

INDEX – AUTHOR, ILLUSTRATOR, TITLE

INDEX – ARTICLES, CONTRIBUTORS AND REVIEWERS

GALWAY COUNTY LIBRARIES